Needs Assessment

_____

P O C K E T   G U I D E S   T O
SOCIAL WORK RESEARCH METHODS

Series Editor
Tony Tripodi, DSW
Professor Emeritus, Ohio State University

Determining Sample Size
Balancing Power, Precision, and Practicality
Patrick Dattalo

Preparing Research Articles
Bruce A. Thyer

Systematic Reviews and Meta-Analysis
Julia H. Littell, Jacqueline Corcoran, and Vijayan Pillai

Historical Research
Elizabeth Ann Danto

Confirmatory Factor Analysis
Donna Harrington

Randomized Controlled Trials
Design and Implementation for
Community-Based Psychosocial Interventions
Phyllis Solomon, Mary M. Cavanaugh, and Jeffrey Draine

Needs Assessment
David Royse, Michele Staton-Tindall, Karen Badger, and
J. Matthew Webster

DAVID ROYSE
MICHELE STATON-TINDALL
KAREN BADGER
J. MATTHEW WEBSTER

Needs Assessment

OXFORD
UNIVERSITY PRESS
2009

OXFORD
UNIVERSITY PRESS

Oxford University Press, Inc., publishes works that further
Oxford University's objective of excellence
in research, scholarship, and education.

Oxford   New York
Auckland   Cape Town   Dar es Salaam   Hong Kong   Karachi
Kuala Lumpur   Madrid   Melbourne   Mexico City   Nairobi
New Delhi   Shanghai   Taipei   Toronto

With offices in
Argentina   Austria   Brazil   Chile   Czech Republic   France   Greece
Guatemala   Hungary   Italy   Japan   Poland   Portugal   Singapore
South Korea   Switzerland   Thailand   Turkey   Ukraine   Vietnam

Copyright © 2009 Oxford University Press, Inc.

Published by Oxford University Press, Inc.
198 Madison Avenue, New York, New York 10016
www.oup.com

Oxford is a registered trademark of Oxford University Press.

Library of Congress Cataloging-in-Publication Data
Needs assessment / David Royse ... [et al.].
p. cm. — (Pocket guides to social work research methods; 8)
Includes bibliographical references and index.
ISBN 978-0-19-536878-9 1. Social case work—Methodology. 2. Social
case work—Evaluation. 3. Needs assessment. I. Royse, David D. (David Daniel)
HV43.N38 2009
361.3'2—dc22
2008030808

Printed in the United States of America
on acid-free paper

Contents

Needs Assessment

1

What Is Needs Assessment?

In this chapter we will examine a concise definition of needs assessment, looking at each of its component parts. We'll consider what the term can imply to different audiences and individuals. Along the way, the reader will learn about different ways to conceptualize need, how needs assessment fits into an organizational context, and how it is used in social service agencies.

Defining Needs Assessment

Simply stated, needs assessment is a process that attempts to estimate deficiencies. The interesting thing about this definition is that the following variations are also good, brief descriptions of the term.

- Needs assessment is a *method* used to estimate *deficiencies*.
- Needs assessment is any *effort* that attempts to determine need.
- Needs assessment is an *activity* that gages *gaps and insufficiencies*.

There are many more variations of these definitions that we could spin off. For example, we could substitute "procedure" for process in the first definition. Or, we could swap words among the four variations; however, it is important for you to realize, first of all, that needs assessment comes about from some action or activity. It is not something that can be produced without someone or, more usually, many people involved. Second, needs assessments provide estimates or sophisticated guesses about perceived needs.

Although it is possible to find professional literature that focuses on the clinical needs assessment of an individual or a family, this book's focus will not be on the microlevel. We will *not* be discussing the use of a battery of psychological tests to determine a diagnosis or the best treatment plan for a client whose needs are problematic. Similarly, we will not be using the term *needs assessment* as applied to a single family and diagnosing their issues.

Instead, our use of the term *needs assessment* will *always* involve an appraisal of some kind of a community or large group. For a macrotype of example, let's consider a large nearby city. Large cities often have wonderfully unique sections or neighborhoods, and these may have entirely different needs. One area that receives a lot of tourists may be concerned with traffic flow and parking, whereas another neighborhood may be most concerned with safety issues because of drive-by shootings and drug sales. The residents of one neighborhood may feel that police and fire protection are adequate and may just want to beautify the parks and common areas with flowers and trees.

It is logical to expect that the residents of different neighborhoods could have divergent views regarding what their neighborhoods most need. (Note that we are not saying in this example that *everyone* is in complete agreement, but that the view represents a sizeable proportion of the neighborhood. Perhaps the neighborhood wanting to improve the streets and traffic flow is a view represented by only 38% of those living there—but that is a larger percentage than those expressing safety concerns or strong opinions about potholes in the street or other problems).

However, communities do not always mean neighborhoods or cities. A community could be comprised of social workers employed in the same hospital or mental health center, a pool of substance abuse counselors interested in continuing education, resident advisors in a large university preparing for the incoming fall class, a company of combat soldiers returning from Iraq, or disaster victims approaching a Red Cross contact center.

Need Is a Relative Term

A key principle in understanding needs assessment is that "need" is a relative term. What does that mean? Let's say that the mayor of your community asks you to consult with the city council and prepare a report that assesses the housing needs in your city. Furthermore, let's assume that just that very morning on the way to work you walked past two apparently homeless women and a homeless man sitting on the curb. It would be natural to think that perhaps the first priority would be to identify how many homeless are being housed in the city's shelters each evening. Perhaps your mind would begin to think about a strategy for counting the homeless who sleep each evening in the city's parks or in the woods beside the river because some of them prefer the outdoors or have disorders that prevent them from wanting to interact socially with others.

Then as you walk into the next block, where there are a lot of apartments for low-income families, your eye catches a fluttering of laundry that someone has hung out to dry and you begin to think that the problem of housing needs must also extend to counting the number of families who live in apartments that are much too small for them. How many apartments, you wonder, have large families crammed into one or two bedrooms? And from there, your mind jumps to the problem of elderly individuals who live in walk-up apartments without elevators, and you wonder how many of them might have arthritis or other mobility conditions.

It is summertime and a young boy who had been playing with a ball on the sidewalk dodges a car to retrieve it from the street. Now you are thinking that even if the boy and his family are "adequately" housed in terms of enough space, if you were to interview him or his parents, they may say that having a backyard to play in or a playground nearby would be at the top of their housing priorities. And that thought leads you to remember a dreadful apartment that you rented when you were an undergraduate working your way through college. It had a small kitchen in the living room, a bedroom, and bath. The heat worked too well, and there was no way to control it. There was no air conditioning in the summer, and the water coming out of the faucet always looked rusty, so you were afraid to drink it. Although you never had a problem with roaches, the tenants in other parts of the building were constantly fighting them. It then occurs to you that it is not so much the interior space that is important but dependable heating and cooling systems and an environment that is free of pests such as insects and rats.

You grab a cup of coffee to ponder all the directions that this assessment of housing needs in the community could take when your friend Denita walks in. As you begin to share your thoughts from your morning walk, she interrupts you with a comment that she has been looking for a new place to live. She is tired of where she lives and *must* have a place that is lovelier. She wants something more contemporary, with a fireplace so that she can get all cozy with a book and a cup of chai tea when it snows. And although she is a single person, she wants a four-bedroom apartment with about 2,400 square feet. She wants enough room to have a home office, a room for watching television with friends, a guest bedroom, and a spacious bedroom for herself. She thinks a minimum of two bathrooms would be necessary, although three would be okay too. Ideally, she would like to be in an apartment complex that has its own pool and exercise room with high-quality equipment.

From this brief vignette, we can see that housing needs can be defined in various ways. Housing needs can be viewed in terms of:

- Persons without any housing
- Persons living in substandard housing because of inadequate space or heating/cooling systems, pests, etc.
- Persons without handicap accessibility
- Persons desiring more aesthetic environments or more amenities

Therefore, when discussing needs assessment you must always be cognizant of the fact that what is "needed" is relative and depends on one's vantage point. Obviously, a hierarchy of need can be constructed from the housing example. Persons who are homeless may be happy to accept even substandard quarters as an improvement in their situation. Safety considerations or access issues might offset square footage, and so forth. It should not be surprising that someone with a lot of disposable income can have an entirely different set of expectations and "needs" when the topic of housing is introduced.

Not only is perception of need based on one's relative wealth or impoverishment, what is viewed as a "need" changes over time. Prior to the invention and widespread adoption of cell phones, many homes had only a single phone that all the members of the family had to share. Now, it is quite common for every member of the family to have his or her own cell phone. Similarly, in 1970, the number of televisions per home was 1.4, and by 2005 the average number was 2.6 per home. Computers have had the same kind of growth; they were virtually nonexistent in 1970, were found in 37% of homes in 1997, and were found in 62% of homes in 2003 (U.S. Census Bureau, 2007). "Need" for a computer was a nonexistent problem until they became marketed to the public at an affordable price. Today many Americans may have an older personal computer but want ("need") a faster model or a laptop. They may also want to do away with that bulky monitor and get a flatscreen. Of course, that "need" is different from the high school student in a rural area who does not have a personal computer or laptop in her home and must travel 18 miles to the nearest library to use one.

Assessment Defined

In the bulleted examples, the term assessment was used as a synonym for gaging and estimating. But sometimes our choice of words can limit the way we think. For example, we might *estimate* how tall a building is or intuitively judge how fast a car is traveling past us on the highway. Both of these examples involve minimal activity on our part and could be wild guesses (not arrived at very objectively or scientifically). That is *not* how we want you to think about needs assessment. A better way to reframe assessment is to think of it as counting.

Continuing with our homeless example, one might conduct a needs assessment to count how many homeless people are staying in the city's shelters each night with the objective of learning whether the number of beds available for them is sufficient. How many have to be turned away or have to sleep on the floor of the dining room? If the demand is consistently greater than the facility can manage, then a need may exist to expand the current shelter or to build a new one.

Counting is the basic task of needs assessment. However, we can also conceive of needs assessment as a specialized type of evaluation. At times, it might be productive to think of it as a feasibility study or "front-end" assessment. Let's say that an out-of-state organization has developed a new residential treatment program for adolescent substance abusers and believes that Midwestern City, with a population of 180,000, will be large enough to provide a sufficient number of referrals to keep the planned 20-bed facility filled. Before the agency goes to the expense and trouble of building the facility and acquiring the necessary permits and certificates to begin operation, it would be helpful for the agency to know if substance abuse counselors in the region: *(a)* feel there is a need for a new residential treatment facility and *(b)* if they would refer clients to it. (And, wouldn't you want to know *how many* clients each therapist would be likely to refer in a year's time?)

In the business world, this type of needs assessment might be known as a market analysis and could examine the viability of the proposed project in terms of its cost, legal feasibility, and any unique environmental or cultural issues that might prevent the project from being successful in that particular market. (For instance, perhaps the drug abuse counselors in the region have a long history of retaining their clients and not referring them to residential services. Or, perhaps they as a group are primarily of the opinion that the residential facility 50 miles away in River City does a great job and they cannot imagine referring clients anywhere else.)

Although counting may be the main way in which needs assessments are conducted, that is not to say that counting is the only way to conduct one. For example, it would be possible to hire an expert who has written extensively on the problem of alcohol treatment and ask that person to consult with a community planning group. That expert may have knowledge derived from needs assessments conducted in other communities and may be able to apply formulae for estimating the amount of service (e.g., outpatient, short-term residential, aftercare) needed in a community from available social indicators such as DWI arrests, deaths from cirrhosis of the liver, and alcohol sales (for a more technical article, see Rush, 1990; Cook & Oei, 1998; Best, Day & Campbell, 2007; see Sawicki & Flynn, 1996).

Ways to Conceptualize Needs Assessment

Bradshaw's Typology

Having options in life (e.g., ice cream comes in more than one flavor) is usually a good thing, and it turns out that use of an expert is just one way to think about conceptualizing a needs assessment. In fact, following Bradshaw's (1977) model, need may be conceptualized as being of four types: normative, expressed, felt, and comparative. Each of these will be discussed.

The use of experts or *key informants* (persons well-positioned in a community to know about it and its problems—sometimes formed into a "blue ribbon" study group) is a particular type of needs assessment methodology or approach known as *normative need*. For a straightforward, simple example, the Mayo Clinic recommends that boys and girls ages 4 to 8 years receive 800 mg of calcium a day. Girls that age need at least 1,200 to 1,800 calories and boys need at least 1,400 to 2,000 and maybe more depending on activity level and age (www.mayclinic.com/health/nutrition-for-kids/NU00606). Children receiving fewer than the recommended levels of calcium or calories would have deficiencies and be in a state of need.

Another way to conceptualize needs assessment is as *expressed need*. Expressed need is based on an examination of clients' requests for services. For example, how many clients did the homeless shelter serve last year and the preceding 3 years? How many of these were young men under the age of 30 years? How many were veterans? How many had visited the shelter on a previous occasion? How many requested a referral to the alcohol treatment unit? Expressed need data will indicate how many were served in the sense of the visible or known clients. However, it might also represent the "tip of the iceberg." It doesn't reveal how many more might need the service who didn't know about the service, couldn't travel there to obtain the service, or who didn't bother to request it for some unknown reason (e.g., they suspected the service might have a long waiting list or require documentation of some kind).

Felt need is the category Bradshaw applied to efforts that directly ask clients what they believe or feel that they need. This is the form of needs assessment that best captures the clients' perspective. Generally speaking, clients would be surveyed or interviewed to learn about their felt needs.

Comparative need is similar to case finding. This category of needs assessment efforts examines the characteristics of those receiving services from a program or agency and then looks for these characteristics elsewhere in the population to extend service and estimate the "true" amount of need if there were no barriers.

What the various ways that need may be conceptualized mean to the student or practitioner trying to understand the term is this: need is a term without conceptual boundaries that must be operationally defined in each usage (Royse, 1982). In other words, because others may not understand what type of need you are concerned about or how you will go about conducting your needs assessment, it is of paramount importance that you and the others on the needs assessment planning team or committee share a common vision and understanding and be able to articulate it to others.

Whether you think about needs assessment as simply counting clients requesting service or a more sophisticated, multipronged effort, underlying the assessment process is an interest in comprehending what the actual needs of a community are. To understand the extent or severity of needs in a community, it is necessary to talk about measuring them. Measurement in a needs assessment can be quantitative or impressionistic. We will discuss these more and return to this topic later, but first we must decide on what should be counted or measured.

Focusing the Needs Assessment: Four Focal Points

Whenever we assess needs, our activity is designed to *measure* the extent of need within the group or community from which we are collecting data. But before we can measure something, we must be clear on what we want to measure. Let's continue to examine ways to conceptualize need by focusing on the problem of what we want to measure. Our attention will be on another four ways to think about need for services in a community.

Awareness of Services

Perhaps the first consideration when looking at social services in the community is the simple question: "Do the residents know that service XYZ exists?" When one is a social worker or a social work student, it is easy to forget that services we know about and expect to find in a community may not be knowledge held by every adult. For example, many adults may not know that affordable services are available for those who need counseling for a substance abuse or mental health problem. In one case study of a county that attempted to keep the public informed about mental health services, 39% of adults in the county did not know if a person with a drug or drinking problem could get counseling within the county, 49% did not know if a couple having marital problems could get counseling, and 53% did not know if counseling was available for children who were not getting along well in school or within their own families (Royse, 1987). Clearly, if services exist but are not visible or known to residents, then the need may be for a public relations campaign rather than the creation of a whole new agency.

Availability of Services

If contacted in a survey, community respondents may know (or guess) that certain services exist within their community without knowing much about their availability (because they have never used the services themselves). For instance, we may know that the local hospital has an emergency department but have very little information about how long we might have to wait if we go there for our sore throat. Or, to take another example, let's say that based on a client's experience in attempting to obtain a mammogram from the public health department—she is told there is a 3-month wait—you have reason to believe that although mammograms are theoretically available, the delay in obtaining them makes them actually somewhat unavailable to someone without insurance worried about a lump in her breast. Availability of services usually refers to the adequacy of the supply of services such as specialized care providers and programs (Penchansky & Thomas, 1981).

Accessibility of Services

Accessibility often has to do with the physical location of services. A very real problem is that those who do not have a car and cannot drive may not be able to travel some distance to receive services. Although the residents may know that the services are available and that they are eligible to receive them, lack of transportation, high gas prices, or comfort level in driving in an unfamiliar part of the city may prevent their accessing services. Other than locations that might present transportation issues for area residents, accessibility issues include:

• Inconvenient hours of operation (e.g., services might be available only from 8 a.m. to 4 p.m. on Monday through Friday, when potential clients who work full-time or go to school might need appointments in the evening or Saturday)
• Lack of staff or facilities to meet the needs of special populations (those deaf, blind, with mobility issues, or needing a translator)
• Fee for services. Even though nominal fees may be collected from clients, even small charges might preclude some clients from being able to access services or prevent others from accessing services from private providers.
• Eligibility for services based on income, age, or geographic boundaries
• Need for child care or adult respite services

Residents of a community may not perceive that services exist for them because of accessibility issues; even if they know or recognize that services are available, they still may perceive a need if the services are viewed as unacceptable.

Acceptability of Services

If services are not perceived as *acceptable*, they may be viewed as being nonexistent when, in fact, they are available and accessible. Generally, acceptability of services can be thought of as the clients' attitudes about the characteristics of the providers and their practices and their perceived attitudes regarding potential clients (Penchansky & Thomas, 1981). What features would make a service unacceptable? Here are a few examples:

- Location in a neighborhood perceived as unsafe
- Staff perceived as incompetent or unprofessional (e.g., staff who might tell others in the community about the resident's problems)
- Staff perceived as unfriendly (or as culturally or ethnically "not like me")
- Perception that the services are too expensive
- Perception that too much paperwork, documentation, or special referral is required
- Long lines or waiting list
- Incongruent values (e.g., unplanned pregnancy and agency won't discuss options other than adoption)
- Dirty
- Lack of privacy
- Demeaning process (e.g., personal, detailed questions)

Sometimes the four different foci seem to be interrelated and difficult to tease apart. For example, inconvenient hours of operation can be viewed as an *accessibility* issue (e.g., if they aren't open in the evenings I can't get an appointment) but might also be viewed as an *acceptability* issue (e.g., I could make a late afternoon appointment, but I prefer evening hours so that I don't have to ask for the time off). Similarly, a potential client with very limited funds who can't *access* services that require a copayment might also say that services that charge too high a fee for services are *not acceptable*.

As you can see from this discussion, there are numerous ways to conceptualize the need for social services in a community. But it does not matter whether our focus is on awareness, availability, accessibility, or acceptability; the purpose of a needs assessment is to obtain an understanding of the extent of the service gaps found in the community being examined. If we think of social services as a safety net to catch those experiencing difficulties in life, then their needs are the holes in the net and assessment is the locating of the holes so that the net can be repaired and made more complete. The purpose of needs assessment is to identify the gaps—generally in a community's service delivery system—although as we will see later in the book, needs assessments can also be conducted on a statewide basis and on a much smaller scale (e.g., staff within a single organization).

In many communities, the local United Way may have created a services directory or services inventory that lists the social and human services available in that county or geographical region. This document could be a useful starting place in identifying just what services are available in the community. The directory or inventory may also contain some accessibility information. However, it is unlikely that you will find awareness or acceptability information there.

As you consider the different ways that needs assessment has been discussed, it may occur to you that the four foci of awareness, availability, accessibility, and acceptability of services each provide an important view from the client's perspective.

How Needs Assessment Fits into an Organizational Context

Most often when we think of social services, we think of those that already exist. Like the clean drinking water that comes out of the tap, they are always available to us. We probably do not think about a time before they existed. However, sometimes social problems seem to occur almost overnight or arise because some careful observer discovered a trend or pattern and brought the problem to the public's attention (e.g., Sudden Infant Death Syndrome, electronic bullying). A single tragedy experienced by a loved one, friend, or family member can also be the catalyst for some new program (Mothers Against Drunk Drivers). Social problems, then, can have roots that can be very recent or be traced back as far as records have been kept.

To be clear, social problems affect large numbers of people and are such difficulties and troubles as alcoholism/drug addiction, homelessness, mental illness, domestic partner and child abuse—to name just a few. They create hardships and suffering for those immediately affected as well as present costs for society that must fund treatment and rehabilitation programs. The existence of social problems leads to the creation of social service organizations and specialized programs to address the problems.

In an idealized environment, planners would have the time and resources needed to conduct a needs assessment to gauge the extent and severity of the problem soon after it comes to light or is identified. Once the magnitude of the problem is known, then planners and service providers can begin to discuss the type of intervention that would stand the best chance of reducing or impacting the problem. Following an evidence-based practice model, it may take months to examine the literature and to discuss how to tackle the problem. Committees trying to find the most effective strategy may decide to take features of several programs and then design a totally new intervention. The economic resources available may ultimately decide which program or intervention is finally implemented because a new program could require additional space and hiring of new staff or retraining of the old.

Once services are in place and operational, evaluation of the effort can inform decision-makers about whether the intervention is making a difference in the community so that the intervention can be fine-tuned if necessary. Good management dictates the collection of evaluative information so that the new program can be finely tuned if it seems to working reasonable well or cancelled if it seems that clients are no better off or are harmed. Sometimes evaluation occurs formally (e.g., an evaluator is hired or given the assignment to determine the success or effectiveness of a program), and sometimes the evaluation is much more informal.

And, after some time passes, the needs of the population should be assessed again to determine how the program has impacted social problems and the needs of the community. If the needs have changed remarkably or perhaps not at all, it may be necessary to engage once more in discussion about the intervention designed to combat the social problem, and thus, the process begins all over again.

A schematic of this process might resemble something like this:

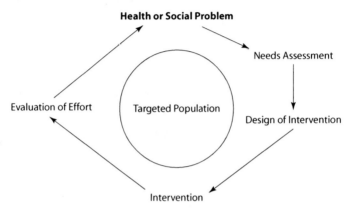

Figure 1.1 Social Service Program Life Cycle

Ideally, every new or redesigned program should start with a needs assessment to allow the intervention to be maximally effective by providing the basic information concerning who has the problem, how many there are, and such specifics as how long have they had the problem, what remedies have been applied, and so forth. The needs assessment at the front of the program life cycle allows for the target population to be clearly and precisely identified so that the intervention has the best chance of success.

Needs assessment always involves a problem focus. The problem may be quite specific where the needs assessment may involve counting the number of reported problems or cases (e.g., child abuse) within a city or state. Or, the needs assessment focus could be population-centered or location-specific in a broad way—as in trying to determine the needs of the survivors of Hurricane Katrina who, besides being homeless, lost their jobs, their pets, their clothing, their neighborhoods and schools, and so forth.

If what you want to know is less about a community or special group and the problem doesn't have a direct impact on clients or social services, then it may be that your interest is not in conducting a needs assessment but some form of basic research. Scientists often ask "why" or "what" questions that are not related to needs assessment. A chemistry student may want to know why dropping Mentos mints into a bottle of Diet Coke produces an instant fountain of spray. What other candies might produce a similar effect? These and other more serious chemistry questions are distinguished from needs assessment questions because in basic science investigations the goal maybe be to answer a question for which there is no immediate use for the knowledge. By contrast, needs assessment always involves an application of the knowledge. Needs assessment starts with a problem to be addressed to improve the quality of life or living conditions of human beings who are often the clients or patients of social workers.

Use of Needs Assessment

There are typically four different ways that needs assessments are used by social workers. Each of these will be discussed in turn.

Securing Resources/Establishing the Need for New Efforts

As already mentioned, needs assessments are often conducted because there is a perception by one or more people in the community that there is a need for a new program, intervention, or agency. For example, when the local homeless shelter is overflowing each night with more men than it can hold, those who are concerned about the problem may begin to advocate for a new shelter. They may inform the mayor or city council of the situation or try to get the local television station to do a news story to inform the public. At some point, someone may call for a needs assessment that goes beyond just counting the overflow at the shelter.

Advocates may advocate for a single solution (e.g., a new, larger shelter) or argue that the solution to the problem may require several different initiatives. For instance, another perspective is that the community should create more single-room occupancy apartments for those who, with Section 8 assistance, could afford to pay some rent and live independently. Or, a third group may insist that creating more detox beds would be a big boost in getting homeless men off the street. As you can see, the needs assessment in this situation could easily be more involved than just counting the number of homeless turned away from the shelter each evening in December and January. The needs assessment effort increases with complexity as the perceived solution to the problem becomes more involved.

Modification of Policy

In addition to advocating for new programming or facilities, advocates may also advocate for the modification or revision of policy. For example, suppose we change the example from homeless men to homeless women. Let's say that the local women's shelter experiences an increase in the number of women who request a bed and that their policy is simply "first come, first served." Under that policy, women with children who arrive later in the evening may be turned away. However, maybe someone advocates for mothers and their children and argues that the policy should be changed to protect a certain number of beds each evening for women with children—in other words, to give preference to them over single women. A needs assessment in this instance might count the number of times that mothers with children were turned away, how many children were involved, and if these families were able to find other shelter.

Improving Services

Good managers of agencies and their corresponding programs want to know how to improve the services delivered to their clients or constituents. For example, social service program managers might want to identify any barriers that keep their clients from keeping appointments (e.g., childcare services, lack of transportation, etc.), the city council may want to know what problems the citizens of a community want addressed, or the Head Start social worker may want to learn how many of the families in her program need coats for their children.

Needs assessments are also used in other circumstances to improve services. For instance, hospitals may call patients who have had surgery to see how their experience could be improved. Although those efforts are often thought of in connection with consumer or client satisfaction surveys, they overlap with needs assessment efforts to the extent that the purpose of the inquiry is to learn what procedures or experiences should change to make things more agreeable and pleasant for patients/clients. The concern is on unmet patient needs. Similar to an evaluation effort, the needs assessment could reveal that something in the organization may need to change to improve services.

Establish or Strengthen Partnerships

The findings of a needs assessment may lead to the development of a new partner or the strengthening of ties with an old one to create new or improved services for clients. Let's take a situation where staff in charge of the homeless shelter identify a problem for a few of their regular clients: those with chronic or severe medical conditions in need of intravenous therapy cannot receive it because there are no medical personnel in the shelter who can administer the medication. By conducting a needs assessment revealing the number of homeless individuals who are too sick to be on the street and not sick enough to remain in the hospital (e.g., those receiving chemotherapy or radiation treatments for cancer, or recovering from surgery), the staff of the shelter are then able to go to the local health department or nearby hospital and ask their partner for assistance. Several communities across the country have solved the problem when shelters have partnered with health-care organizations and jointly opened a respite center for homeless individuals (*see* http://www.hud.gov/local/tx/homeless/2003-03-20.cfm).

Summary

This chapter has provided the conceptual foundation for understanding the concept of needs assessment. With this groundwork in place, we can now build upon it in the following chapters as we begin to think about planning the needs assessment for our communities or agencies. As we discussed, the first step is with the identification of a problem. The process proceeds through to the writing of a report that can then be disseminated to interested parties. The following figure provides a quick schematic of the steps involved in most needs assessments, although they may vary slightly as we will see in the coming chapters.

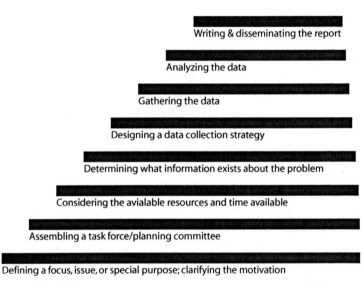

Writing & disseminating the report

Analyzing the data

Gathering the data

Designing a data collection strategy

Determining what information exists about the problem

Considering the avialable resources and time available

Assembling a task force/planning committee

Defining a focus, issue, or special purpose; clarifying the motivation

Figure 1.2 Diagram of Basic Steps in the Needs Assessment Process

2

First Steps in the Needs Assessment Process

Needs assessments vary immensely. This variation can stem from the type of problems that must somehow be assessed, the planned uses of the data collection effort, the resources available, as well as the design and methodology used. There can be many factors affecting the way needs assessments are conducted—so many, in fact, that it is helpful to think about the topic of needs assessment not in terms of a particular recipe that one could always duplicate with success, but in terms of a collection of recipes—or better yet, a continuum of information-gathering approaches. The continuum is a useful construct whether we think about the design rigor or generalizability of the findings, the cost of the effort, the number of participants involved, or other facets. In this chapter, our goal is to introduce the reader to the basic components of the needs assessment planning process. Needs assessments, no matter how complex or simple, must consider many of the same issues, although they may address them in different ways.

Motivation for the Needs Assessment

Using the construct of the continuum in Figure 2.1, we can start by stating that needs assessments can vary in terms of the emotional energy,

Low   Medium   High
Required Efforts   Grassroots Efforts

Figure 2.1 Example of a Needs Assessment Motivation/Commitment Continuum

passion, or commitment associated with them. The case scenario described in the textbox illustrates a relatively low motivational level for those charged with conducting the needs assessment.

The Case of the Mandated Needs Assessment

Years ago, when one of the authors was employed as the director of research and evaluation for a mental health board, the state mental health department required that a needs assessment would be conducted annually in each catchment area. Every mental health board in the state was mandated to conduct a needs assessment but each local board could decide its own methodology, the clientele, or special population to be studied as well as how much effort to put into the project. Thus, one board might contact service providers to determine what new needs or problems were being identified within their clientele; another board might place an ad in the newspaper and have citizens write in their perceived needs and mail the information to the board. A third board might conduct a random survey of persons residing in the community. It seemed as if almost any data collection activity labeled a needs assessment was acceptable to those in the state office.

The required needs assessment felt like busywork instead of a legitimate planning activity that would have been useful to the state and local authorities. On one hand, it is understandable that those requiring a needs assessment effort were probably being sensitive to the fact that some of the local mental health boards were extremely strapped for resources. However, because there were no guidelines directing the local boards to focus on certain clientele or populations (e.g., children, older adults, persons of color, substance abusers, etc.) and no expectation of a standardized methodology (e.g., every board was free to create its own questionnaire and to disseminate it however they wished), the information at the local level would not be comparable to the data collected in the surrounding counties by different mental health boards. In other words, the information being reported "up" to the state officials was going to be spotty and uneven and make it impossible to see the state's mental health needs from a single perspective. In fairness to the state authorities, the required needs assessment was surely an attempt

---

(continued)

The Case of the Mandated Needs Assessment *(continued)*

on their part to encourage local authorities to examine their priorities in terms of what they were going to fund and what they weren't using some kind of a thoughtful, reflective process. Although the governmental authorities were within their rights to mandate needs assessment, it is questionable how much impact that requirement had on the mental health board's actual planning, allocation, and program implementation cycle. What we can say for sure is that dispassionate informational reports were generated. One can't help but wonder if the results might have had a greater impact if the needs assessment originated from a grassroots effort of citizens in the community or if the staff of an agency detected an alarming trend in some problem or a change in demographic or utilization patterns and wanted to advocate for new programming.

On the opposite end of the motivational continuum are those projects where there is a group of very concerned individuals who are vitally involved with a problem. These could be, for example, the family members and friends of individuals in the community who have committed suicide. A recent tragedy could spark the friends and family members to become vocal and passionate advocates for programs for suicide prevention and treatment. Because they are energized and eager to tackle the problem, they may view the needs assessment as the key information needed to bring about the program or the changes they want to see. Often, one or more individuals recognize the importance of having actual data about the incidence and extent of a problem. This information can then be used to apply leverage for increased services or to bring about help for those that they are most concerned about.

Perhaps in the middle of the continuum would be staff or professionals who, in the course of performing their normal jobs, observe a misalignment between clients' needs and where or how an agency has arranged its services. Their main concern is that the scarce resources within an agency or community be correctly targeted toward the populations that have either the most or the most severe needs. These staff may not be passionate about their discovery, but because they are professionals, they want to improve services for clients.

Because their knowledge is based on a handful of cases, they know that a more systematic data collection effort should be conducted. Unlike the parents of children with a developmental disorder or the daughter with a parent needing day respite services, concerned professionals may have no personal investment in lobbying for new or expanded services. Thus, they may be only moderately active or committed in advocating for a specific change in services.

Another example of a needs assessment where there might be no group advocating for a certain outcome, but where there still might be a fair amount of energy for the effort, could be a community where the mayor or other official requests a needs assessment. This might be in response to complaints about the response time of ambulances or police, the problem of potholes in the street, parents who want recreational services or parks for their children. Some sort of community-wide assessment could allow the elected officials to make more informed decisions about problems and how to spend surplus funds or to distinguish small or infrequent problems from those that most citizens consider urgent. Of course, a special interest group could mobilize around an issue such as police using too much force, and these groups could be highly energized.

It should be clear that need assessment efforts vary depending on the motivation and commitment of those involved in the project. A needs assessment committee or task force with strong motivation and energy will be able to accomplish more than a group of citizens with little enthusiasm.

No matter whether the proposed needs assessment effort is one where there is much energy, enthusiasm, or group support or one being conducted quietly by a single staff person, in each instance the purpose for carrying out the needs assessment has to be attuned to the *stakeholders*. Stakeholders consist of anyone who has a connection to the issue or problem. Witkin and Altschuld (1995) distinguish between *primary* stakeholders (program beneficiaries, those whom the program was designed to benefit) and *secondary* stakeholders (those individuals providing the program or who make policies or decisions regarding the program). Thus, if the problem is the recent increase in high school dropouts, the secondary stakeholders could include the superintendent, the principals, guidance counselors, social workers, teachers, the school board, or organized groups of parents as well as taxpayers who vote on school levies and approve construction of new schools. Employers, politicians, and civic leaders who work with school personnel to improve or strengthen the schools could also be considered stakeholders.

If the needs assessment is being conducted within a social service agency, stakeholders logically include clients (past and current), agency staff, as well as others in the community who are concerned (e.g., clergy or other social workers who refer to the agency). Stakeholders are important because they may be the reason a program or intervention exists (e.g., they are clients), they may work for the program (e.g., staff, managers, directors), refer clients to it (e.g., judges, attorneys, social workers), or they see the need for it and may have the clout or the power to facilitate change. Certainly, when the needs assessment is being planned, the task force or committee discussing what type of data to collect should consider who will use the information, who will be reading the report, and perhaps even attempt to anticipate the kinds of questions that the stakeholders will raise about the needs assessment.

Each group of stakeholders may have different interests. Clients, for example, will want more of their needs met by the agency. With limited funds, administrators may want to prioritize the needs of the service population. Advocates for a new program will want to show how their issue is more important or a bigger problem than others. Funders may want to see a needs assessment before committing funds, and so on. For now, it is important to keep in mind that the clout of the stakeholders and their presumed support (or lack of the same) will have an influence on the needs assessment process.

Where Do I Start?

If you are like most social workers or social work students, the first question that probably arises when you are given the responsibility for conducting a needs assessment is "Where do I start?" Fortunately, the process is not like entering a labyrinth where there is a single entry and exit point, nor is it composed of narrow steps along the way that could cause a fatal fall if you slipped and missed one.

As a needs assessment investigator, you may begin your planning by considering any one of several key decision-points. You may think of these issues as gates into the needs assessment planning process. There are multiple "gates" or starting places. To extend this metaphor just a bit more, they can be viewed as differing in size. An agency may be rich in the resources it can devote to the needs assessment or it may be relatively impoverished. Similarly, there could be a generous timeline (a wide gate!) for completion of the project or the data might be needed ASAP, to take just two examples. The next section of this chapter will discuss some of the major components that affect the needs assessment design that you will ultimately decide on.

Purpose and Impact/Utility

The impact/utility of the needs assessment cannot be discussed without talking about purpose. In fact, purpose and impact/utility may be inseparable. Discussion may originate within the agency as staff examine some client issue or discuss future services, but it is also possible that a governing board, a committee, or an administrator could decide that a needs assessment should be conducted. As in the scenario described earlier in the chapter, the mandated needs assessment might come without clear expectations about what data should be gathered or how the data should be utilized. In such situations, those charged with the responsibility for conducting the needs assessment may need to seek additional information before proceeding to the planning stage.

Sometimes the catalyst for a needs assessment comes from a perceived possible problem. The impetus may arise from a dramatic problem brought to the public's attention. However, the problem may affect relatively few people, and the needs assessment may result from relatively few people who are dedicated to advocating for a new program or something broader, such as better police protection, that affects all the citizens in a community. Whatever the motivation, the purpose, desired impact, and use of the needs assessment are a major "gate" or starting point for planning. If you and the committee working on the needs assessment anticipate a skeptical response or perhaps even a hostile rejection of your findings, then it is very likely that you will want to plan the best, most rigorous data collection that you can afford. Even with a small budget, you might need to plan an effort that can stand up to strong scrutiny. (Information is provided in Chapter 3 about the levels of rigor associated with different needs assessment strategies.)

When a group of advocates meet to plan a needs assessment, the topic that might be discussed first could be, "How do we convince XYZ that this is a real problem in the community?" Thus, the starting place of purpose/impact/utility may involve the politics of bringing about change. Change doesn't always come easily—even when well-documented evidence of a problem is presented to rational, intelligent decisionmakers. Because creating a new program may require cutting the budget of one program to divert funds to a new program, there are often strong advocates for protecting the status quo who do not want to see change. Therefore, needs assessments may involve political considerations about who must be convinced and the best way to accomplish that. When starting at this gate, the planners' focus may be on such political issues as:

- What would be the best evidence (or the most credible sources of information) to convince skeptics of need for the desired program?
- What evidence would convince the decisionmakers?
- What evidence would mobilize the community to recognize this problem?

Considerations when planning what data are needed in the political realm may include knowledge that the mayor, for instance, is perceived to be more likely to listen to certain individuals, organizations, or neighborhoods than others. It follows that these influential persons or groups should be included in the needs assessment effort. There is no hard and fast rule about how best to involve them—this will involve one's knowledge of the agency or community, the decisionmakers, and then what data would be most likely to exert the influence needed to result in the desired change.

Every needs assessment must have a purpose. The purpose may be crystal clear (in which case the planning committee can immediately move to discussion of how best to conduct the needs assessment), or it may be somewhat vague. If you are one of the individuals asked to help with the needs assessment planning, it is going to be vitally important to clarify the group's mission so that the needs assessment can be properly focused. Here are some questions to ask the "higher-ups" if the expectations for the needs assessment are unclear.

Ask or seek the answers to questions such as these:

1. Why is the needs assessment being planned at this point in time? (What is the driving motivation behind the needs assessment? Has a particular problem or issue arisen that is the catalyst?)
2. What is the purpose of the needs assessment?
3. Who will use the needs assessment? (Who must be convinced? What data are needed?)
4. How will the needs assessment be used?
5. What do we hope to accomplish with the needs assessment?
6. When is the report needed? (How much urgency is there?)

Of course, there will be other questions that you will want to ask later, but unambiguous responses to these questions would be an enormous step forward.

There is no substitute for knowing what you hope to accomplish with the needs assessment data. Vague, poorly defined objectives will result in a broad mish-mash of unrelated and unfocused information that may turn out to not be all that useful or worth the expenditure of effort to obtain it.

Table 2.1 provides several examples of vague questions and improved, more refined questions that would be helpful in guiding a needs assessment effort.

Vague questions generate responses that will be all over the place with no clear indication of how they relate to services needed. Respondents need a context or frame of reference. If a question is too open, then the

Table 2.1 Examples of Vague and Specific Questions for a Needs Assessment

Vague, Unhelpful Questions	Specific, Targeted Questions
What are the needs in this community?	Do parents of teens support the development of a weekend teen club with supervision by hired staff?
Do citizens in this community have good mental hygiene?	What percent of the adult citizens are depressed (as defined by the CES-D)?*
Is drinking a problem in this community?	What percent of adults say that others have complained about the extent of their drinking?
Are older adults managing okay?	Do the majority of older adults in this city know who to call if they feel they are being mistreated by family members?

* The CES-D is a 20-item self-reporting measure developed by the Center for Epidemiologic Studies, National Institute of Mental Health to measure depressive symptomatology in the general population (Radloff, 1977).

information produced may not be useful. Although it might be informative to learn that potholes in the street are a major concern (which might be a finding with the first vague question), there may not be a lot that an organization such as Big Brothers/Big Sisters or the Salvation Army can do about such problems. The lesson here is to make sure that the questions for which you seek answers relate to the purpose of your needs assessment and fall within your agency's area of responsibility. For example, if the Salvation Army in your community is the largest provider of shelter for the homeless, then a needs assessment originating from them might ask their stakeholders, "When you think about the homeless in this community, what services do they need that do not currently exist?

Resources

Once the purpose of the needs assessment and use of its data have been agreed on, another very important consideration is the amount of money that will be available to conduct the needs assessment. For example, if the agency director has set aside $25,000, then you might be able to hire a polling firm to conduct a scientific statewide poll. If your budget is limited

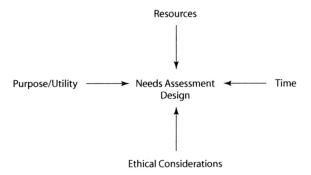

Figure 2.2 Factors Affecting the Needs Assessment Design

to $250, then you could buy box lunches for participants in one or two focus groups or mail out several hundred surveys or perhaps not collect any new data at all but contact other agencies in the community to see what information they may have about the problem.

When you think of the resources at your disposal, you should not think of just the monetary ones. You may have a pool of administrative assistants who can be tapped to make phone calls or to process mailed questionnaires. In large agencies, there may be someone who has expertise with data analysis or drawing stratified random samples. Resources might include use of a large conference or general purpose room for focus groups or community meetings, the ability to make lots of photocopies at no or low cost, unlimited use of the telephone, or staff who are willing to volunteer and assist where you need them. When you are at this "gate," it is a good idea to make a list of all the resources available to the needs assessment effort.

Another possible resource is the information that social service agencies keep on their clients—especially if this information is computerized and can be accessed easily. All manner of demographic information can then be analyzed from street addresses/neighborhoods, to income data, number of children or older adults in the family, presenting problems, and so forth. An agency that has kept good intake, screening, and service data over the years provides the needs assessor with the potential of showing trend data. For example, going back 3–7 years may allow one to see how clients' problems have changed over time. Agency data can be a very important source of information and yet a very affordable one.

If a needs assessment has never been conducted in your geographical region (or at least, a copy cannot be located), a good place to start would be inventorying the social and human services already existing in the county. Check with your local United Way to see if they have already produced a service inventory. There is no reason to advocate for a service or to duplicate one that might already exist but be unknown to you. This services inventory can be done two ways: you can look in the Yellow Pages of your phone directory under such headings as "Social Service Organizations," Mental Health Services," Counseling Services," and "Counselors" and make a list of the organizations and services. However, note that this effort alone will be incomplete because an agency (e.g., Catholic Social Services) may provide a range of programs but have only a single, central phone number listed. Alternatively, you could start with a list of agencies compiled from the phone directory and either call or mail a questionnaire to each, asking them to list all of the programs they provide and other pertinent details (locations, hours of operation, eligibility considerations, etc.) as well as any other similar programs they know about.

If there is a United Way in your community, it would be a good idea to contact staff there to learn what previous needs assessments they have sponsored or conducted in the past. For an example of a United Way that has posted the results of its needs assessments from several past years on the Internet (though based on social indicators supplied from others), go to www.unitedwaydallas.org/CommunityAssessment.

Time

Time is also a resource, because more complex needs assessments can be conducted when there is the luxury of having enough time to plan properly and implement things without frantically rushing to completion. When the needs assessment effort must be completed in short order, it usually cannot be multilayered or complicated in design. (You can read more about design considerations in Chapter 3.) A question you might want answered early in the planning phase is whether you will receive release time from other duties to be in charge of or work on the needs assessment, and if so, how many hours a week.

When considering how much time is available for conducting the needs assessment, one should always create a bit of a "pad" for unexpected contingencies. The print shop could get behind because of a large job or have equipment failure delaying the production of your survey forms. Similarly, you might lose time when a computer with addresses crashes or by learning at the last minute that the post office requires bulk mail presented to them with the addresses arranged by zip code—the delay in getting the addresses sorted might mean that you miss delivery on the day that you had planned. In summary, you should expect some "slippage" of deadlines and allow for unexpected delays and hindrances.

When you begin to list of all the steps involved in creating your needs assessment, it is possible to see several places where delays could be experienced. Realistically estimate how much time is needed for the total needs assessment effort and then multiply that figure by 20% to 30% to allow for the delays and setbacks that will inevitably be experienced.

When you are at this gate, it is important to arrive at a clear understanding of how much time will be required for the needs assessment as well as when the data collection is expected to be finished or the report due.

Ethical Considerations

There are occasions when trying to decide how best to capture needs assessment data could lead to discussion of ethical issues. For example, suppose you are asked to design a needs assessment for the survivors of a large industrial explosion where over 100 factory workers were burned or injured. It would be possible to create a very simple questionnaire using a small number of questions. You might ask something along these lines: (1) Since being injured in the explosion, is there anything that you need that you don't currently have?; (2) If you had a magic wand that could grant you three wishes, what would you wish for?; or, (3) Is there anything you need to rehabilitate you to the same level of functioning that you had before the factory explosion?

The unfortunate thing about all three of these questions is that they might create an expectation in the respondents that they will receive or should receive outright gifts or remuneration for their suffering. The questions might make some respondents think about how if they had a new flat screen television, a new SUV, or a vacation in Bermuda to recover, then they could be so much happier. However, this probably would not have been the intention of the mental health center that was simply trying to determine if those who were injured were aware that individual and group counseling were available to help them to rehabilitate. Along this line, the community United Way might have constructed questions like these when the agency was really trying to decide whether to allocate additional funding to a special job-training or employment service for those who were badly injured. To avoid setting up a situation that might generate unrealistic expectations or false hope in respondents, those involved in planning a needs assessment of the survivors of the factory explosion would need to be very careful and sensitive in drawing up the questions they want to ask so that respondents are not mislead about the purpose of the needs assessment. In fact, it is entirely possible that some groups planning a needs assessment effort might start with a discussion of how to present the data collection without misrepresenting or giving a false notion.

Ethical issues also arise if you are asking sensitive information. Consider these examples:

- You are working for a Planned Parenthood agency and want to go into the sophomore class of the local high school to ask if the teens are using safe sex practices and know where to obtain condoms.
- You are working for an outpatient substance abuse treatment agency and want to know how many bus drivers drink on the job.
- You are working for a community mental health agency and want to know how often police officers are abusive toward their family members and if they view themselves as being "stressed out."

Information about illegal behavior or behavior that could potentially cause someone to lose his or her job or to get into trouble always raises ethical concerns. To protect the rights of human research subjects, every college and university (as well as hospitals and other organizations that receive federal funds) must have an *Institutional Review Board (IRB)*. Researchers must submit their proposed research plans (their *protocols*) to the appropriate IRB for review. IRBs are empowered to grant approval for the research to be conducted or to reject the plan. If there are problems, the IRB may ask the researcher to modify the data collection procedure, to present each potential participant with a letter explaining the study, or even ask for a consent document signed by the participant that acknowledges the risk of participating. Usually, IRBs recommend that service providers not collect data from their clients themselves so that clients do not feel coerced. That is, clients could feel that they have to cooperate with the needs assessment so that they won't jeopardize the services that they are receiving.

Although every IRB has the same charge and mission, they do vary somewhat in what they might expect from a student's project. Although as a student you may feel that your needs assessment does not place the participants at risk, you still need to contact your college or university IRB to see if they would recommend that you submit an application to them seeking approval for the study. IRBs often require that students have a faculty advisor or sponsor. Generally speaking, IRBs will want to review your protocol if you are planning on submitting your study for a public presentation or writing it up for a professional journal. If you are an agency employee or a consultant for an agency, then check with the administrative staff there to determine whether the agency has its own IRB. If it does not, but you plan on obtaining needs assessment data that may be of a sensitive or risky nature, then the college or university in your area might be willing to review your protocol.

Creating a Needs Assessment Planning Team

Okay, you've been asked to organize a needs assessment effort and you have a good understanding of its purpose, the budget at your disposal, and how long you have to finish the project. You will need some help, of course; who should you ask or recommend be appointed to be a part of a needs assessment planning team? Rather than specific individuals, it makes the most sense to think in terms of the skills or talents that you will need. A "dream team" might consist of individuals in all of the following roles. Once again, however, the type of needs assessment being planned and the resources available will affect the final composition of the team.

☐ Someone who is willing to be the *convener* or facilitator of the committee.

In this role the team member will set meeting dates, send notices, guide discussion, keep track of assignments, and generally keep the group focused on completing the project.

☐ One who is reasonably well-informed about survey procedures/ methodologies.

This role is especially important if your team decides to conduct a community or client population survey to survey key informants or service providers. The team member should know about the strengths and weaknesses associated with different types of surveys (discussed more in Chapter 3), should be able to construct a random selection process, and should be knowledgeable about questionnaire design.

☐ An assistant who can help with word processing, duplicating, stuffing envelopes, and who is knowledgeable about mailing processes. Even if you don't use a mailed survey, you will very likely need administrative support for typing letters, making appointments for phone contacts, or seeing that questionnaires are distributed as planned to the targeted clients/consumers.

☐ A team member who is knowledgeable of the key players in the community and the agency—one who is politically savvy. This team member's responsibility is to keep the needs assessment out of trouble. For example, in a large agency, there may be one staff member with considerable clout who should not be overlooked if staff members are being polled. This team member's job is to make sure that anyone who might be in a position to discredit or be negative about the needs assessment is consulted or educated sufficiently about the project to allow them to feel included. This team member should not be new to the agency or the community but a "seasoned pro" whose clear thinking and knowledge of key personalities will determine who to go to solve problems that may arise.

☐ At least one and preferably two team members who can be counted on to do the physical work associated with the conduct of the needs assessment. These individuals may be needed to make numerous phone calls if a telephone survey approach is chosen, to help tabulate the results of a large mailed survey effort, or to help by conducting or recording the content of focus group discussions.

☐ Someone comfortable with writing the results obtained from the needs assessment. This team member need not be a journalist or anyone who has written for professional journals but could be the person in the agency who writes the agency newsletter, press releases, or development letters. Besides knowledge of good grammar and an easy to read writing style, it is important that this person have the ability to write an executive summary and be able to assist with writing or editing a more lengthy report from the data that the needs assessment team could provide.

In selecting possible team members, two rules should be followed. First, choose only those who are known to be dependable, conscientious individuals. You do *not* need the aggravation of a team member who cannot be counted on—those who disappear when there is actual work to be done. If individuals you don't know volunteer or are nominated to serve on the committee, check their references before accepting them or giving them a crucial role on the planning team. Some people are not well-suited to work on committees because they compete with others or the facilitator for leadership, are negative, or slow the group down by continually having it go back and review plans already decided on in previous meetings. Try to avoid these individuals.

Second, keep in mind that adding more people to the planning team does not necessarily mean that the work of the team will get done any quicker. In other words, five or six members may be an optimal planning team. As you add more members, discussions will involve more points of view and may lengthen the time that it takes to come to a decision. Committees can become too large and drag down the whole process.

Although it is entirely possible that you, as an individual, are quite capable of conducting a needs assessment on your own without involving a team or committee, we are of the opinion that "two heads are better than one" and encourage any sole researcher to involve others "in the know" and to create a needs assessment team or task force. The feedback you receive regarding your plans can improve your needs assessment and make it more targeted, appropriate, and maximally informative. A second benefit of inviting others is that they share in the product and recognition. We will discuss the concept of "buy-in" in more detail in Chapter 6, but for now we suggest that it is usually better to have the needs assessment be a "team effort" than the work of the "lone ranger." Even with limited resources, you might try to convene a "blue-ribbon" panel of experts for the needs assessment team who are well-known and respected in the community. These could be the heads of social service agencies, politicians, clergy, physicians, judges, and perhaps university faculty. This group could be asked to guide the needs assessment effort, to raise funds for it, or simply to review the final report and add their support to its findings. A blue-ribbon panel is usually recommended when the needs assessment is likely to reveal major problems or is of a sensitive nature. The prestige of the group provides protection from those who might want to discount its findings.

Needs Assessment Checklist

This chapter has contained a lot of valuable information about starting a needs assessment. To assist you with applying this information when you must actually conduct a needs assessment, the following checklist has been prepared.

Needs Assessment Checklist

☐ The purpose of the needs assessment is clear and
well-understood

☐ Sufficient resources are available

☐ The amount of time allowed for the project is adequate

⊓ There are no ethical problems or issues

☐ The target population is well-defined

☐ The methodology for the needs assessment:

(a) is fully supported by the planning team
(b) is going to provide the data needed
(c) is rigorous enough for the audience

☐ Help is available for drawing the sample (if necessary)

☐ Assistance with questionnaire design or identification of
standardized scales can be found

☐ Expertise for interpreting and analyzing the data is available

☐ Help is available for writing the final report, executive summary,
and publicizing the findings

Examples of Needs Assessments on the Web

United Way of Central Alabama (**www.uwca.org/initatives1.html**)
A 2006 report on seven health and human service issues and five
counties

United Way of Inland Valley (**www.uwiv.org/_help/needs_assess-
ment.html**)
Twelve different regions in California are profiled in this report.

United Way of Marion County West Virginia (**www.uwmarion.org/
needs.htm**)
A 2003 PowerPoint presentation that drew upon five focus groups

United Way of Lane County, Oregon (**www.unitedwaylane.org/_Assets/
PDFFILES/07CommAssetsReport.pdf**)

A 2007 report drawing upon over 1,000 telephone interviews
United Way of Will County, Illinois (**www.unitedwaywillcounty
.org/uwwc%20assessment.pdf**)
A 2006 report involving 220 in focus groups, 5000 in a random
community survey, and individuals calling into a 24-hour
crisis line.

3

Selecting a Needs
Assessment Design

This chapter will present a range of needs assessment data collection methods organized from the least to most intensive depending on needed time, resources, and expertise. For instance, social service organizations with very limited financial and staffing resources may opt to review existing and secondary data sources (including agency records or the U.S. census) to identify selected populations for targeting. Locating appropriate social indicators suggestive of possible need might also be useful, as well as appealing, to those on a shoestring budget. An impressionistic approach (e.g., use of focus groups) is an option, whereas observation of a particular group or agency is another way of capturing valuable information. Still others may wish to conduct surveys of their current or prospective clients or citizens in the community. This chapter will explain these methods and provide guidance concerning the strengths and weaknesses of the various needs assessment approaches.

Choosing the Right Design

As discussed in Chapter 1, needs assessment is a vital part of the social service program life cycle that comes at the "front end" of program development and is followed by program implementation and then evaluation. It can be thought of as the beginning part of the evaluation process. Indeed, besides "Does the program work as intended?," a crucial question for every program evaluation should be "Does the program provide what the clients need?" Similarly to program evaluation efforts, needs assessments are focused on a *specific* population, clientele, or community problem and are not expected to provide generalizable information that characterizes basic science research. That is, the needs assessor is not interested in creating scientific principles that can be used across America or by every social scientist. Generally, the findings are often only going to be applicable at a local agency or community level.

Keeping this in mind, there is not going to be a single design that will fit every community or setting. The right design will depend on the variables that have influenced the needs assessment, the resources, and what information the planners hope to take from the effort. Community A will almost inevitably have a different needs assessment design than Community B, and that is okay because the problems in their communities are not the same and they want to know different things. Designs are not produced in "cookie-cutter" fashion as much as they are drafted, revised, tailored, and shaped. There is no single "right" design, and there are very few "wrong" designs. It is best to think of needs assessments as running along a continuum in the same way that program evaluation can be on a continuum from most rigorous to least rigorous.

Choosing the right design is important because it guides the overall approach and structures the questions to be addressed, the data to be collected, the data analysis, and the conclusions and interpretations can be drawn from the data in the final report. There are numerous designs that can be used to conduct a needs assessment project. Choosing the right one is somewhat analogous to buying a new entertainment system. The primary consideration may be how much money you have to spend. Similarly, the needs assessment researcher must also consider how much has been budgeted for the project and the scope of the question or questions that can be answered by the project. Budgets for needs assessment projects may be very limited—release time for one social worker of 4 hours a week or $500 in agency funds to determine how the agency's work environment can be improved to allow for a healthier balance between work and family life. On the other end of the spectrum may be a project that secured major federal funding to conduct a needs assessment on the health problems experienced by children living in poverty in a given geographical area. Design issues have to be considered relative to financial constraints, including the use of staff time for collecting data (such as conducting phone interviews or making follow-up contacts with clients in person); postage, telephone, or travel expenses; purchase of copyrighted instruments or scales; the amount of time required to write the report; and so on. These and other types of factors contribute to the overall cost of the needs assessment project and the subsequent decisions about a needs assessment design.

Whereas the entertainment center shopper must consider whether a DVD player and surround sound are really necessary, the needs assessment researcher must decide which components of the project are essential to answer the primary questions. For example, the needs assessment researcher may believe that the best way to get an accurate representation of the views of foster care parents on needed health care for their children is to conduct a large probability survey of all foster care parents in the state. Depending on the financial resources for the project, this decision may have to be weighed against a more cost-efficient targeted survey to a randomly selected group of foster care parents living in a particular city.

Besides the issue of cost, shoppers and needs assessment researchers must simultaneously consider other factors. For example, although the entertainment center shopper may consider the warranty on the equipment purchase, the needs assessment researcher must give thought to the amount of time that he or she has available to conduct the study and write up the results. Often, in more rigorous research designs, the more data that are collected, the stronger the study. However, more rigorous research designs may not be necessary to answer specific questions for a needs assessment.

In summary, no one design will be applicable or correct in every situation. As discussed in Chapter 2, the ultimate decision about the needs assessment design depends on: *(1)* the nature of the problem being investigated; *(2)* the availability of data; *(3)* monetary and staff resources;

(4) the amount of time one has to complete the project; and *(5)* the purpose of the needs assessment. Strategies for picking the right design are often developed from the specific objectives of the project and the nature of the presenting problem. It is very important to consider all of these factors during the planning stage so that the chosen design is a good fit to conduct the needs assessment. One would not want to choose a design and then look for a problem to investigate.

Deciding on the Specific "Need" to Address

The focus of a needs assessment is to determine the needs of a particular group or community. The needs assessment design that you choose will need to be possible with the available resources (time, money, expertise) of the individuals or agencies planning to conduct the needs assessment. The needs assessment design must also be appropriate to answer the specific questions that the researchers want to address. For example, if Mental Health Agency Z wants to know the attitudes and opinions of their clients on expanding services to patients who test positive for HIV, there would be little need to survey all the clients in all the mental health agencies across the state to answer this question. The specific question that the researchers are interested in is pertinent to Mental Health Agency Z, and a small targeted survey of clients (and perhaps treatment providers) who participate in services should be able to provide valuable information to address this "need."

The needs assessment "question" should also be focused, targeted, and very specific. The following examples are specific questions that could be addressed in a needs assessment:

- What are the gaps in outpatient services provided by a women's substance abuse treatment agency?
- What are the needs of at-risk children that could be addressed through after school programming at the local YMCA?
- What special training do community mental health providers need to provide better services to prisoners transitioning from the institution to the community?

Examples of research questions that are not directly needs assessment-related include the following:

- What is the relationship between poverty and educational achievement among elementary school children in inner-city neighborhoods?
- What are the significant predictors of burnout among child protective service workers?
- Are there significant differences between rural and urban police officers in response to domestic violence reports?

The difference between these groups of questions is that the first set poses questions to address a particular problem. The second set explores questions about the relationship between variables that would likely be answered through basic scientific research designs. The point is that in choosing the right design for your needs assessment project, you must identify exactly the questions that the study should answer to be sure that a needs assessment design is the best way to proceed.

With the understanding that you have given considerable thought to the available resources and the question(s) to be asked, you are ready to proceed with selecting the right design for your project. The next few sections are presented to guide decisions about design selection with an emphasis placed on time, finances, and expertise.

Focus Groups

The American Heritage Dictionary (2000) defines a focus group as:

"A small group selected from a wider population and sampled, as by open discussion, for its members' opinions about or emotional response to a particular subject or area, used especially in market research or political analysis."

Focus groups are often used in market research, political analysis, and social science research. Focus groups are popular and widely used because they are an inexpensive approach to data gathering for a needs assessment and require little time and little expertise (Tipping, 1998). Focus groups

are considered a flexible tool for gathering information for a needs assessment because they permit open discussion from a group of people,
which often provides lots of great information (Vilela, 2007).

Focus groups lend themselves nicely as a data collection approach for
conducting a needs assessment because they encourage interaction
among participants, which may then result in valuable suggestions or
recommendations as different perspectives are exchanged. An example of
a focus group exchange may go something like this (R = Respondent):

Question: Can you please describe the services you have received in
this program:

- R1: I have participated in parenting classes.
- R2: Yeah, me too. Parenting classes, and also employment services.
- R3: I didn't know they even offered employment services here!
- R2: Yes, Ms. Sue is great. She helped me design a resume, practice a
  job interview, and find clothes to wear. I got the first job I applied
  for!
- R1: I didn't know about these services either—who is your primary
  counselor?
- R2: Susan.
- R3: Ah—that explains it. She is the best one here from what I hear.
  My counselor spends little time with me. She just wants to hurry
  me out the door.

This focus group transcript tells us a couple of very important things
about this agency's programming. First, several of the respondents indicate
that they need employment services. Therefore, increasing the visibility
(and perhaps variety) of employment services at the agency may be an
important needs assessment finding from this group. Second, there seem
to be some differences in services provided by the primary counselors.
As an agency director, this may be very important information. It appears
some clients are being exposed to a broader array of services than others,
which may suggest that staff need to be trained to provide a more consistent referral to employment services.

This example of findings from a focus group transcript illustrates that this approach offers the opportunity to not only hear what group participants may say in response to targeted questions but also to observe discussion and exchanges between clients, which may also yield unexpected but valuable information for the needs assessment project.

Focus groups are typically conducted with 8–12 participants who are representative of the target population that the needs assessment team wants to target. Consider this example: over-the-counter (OTC) syringe sales can create unnecessary problems for pharmacists because of their availability for substance abusers who want to use the syringes for injecting illegal drugs. If a needs assessment team is interested in understanding the problem of OTC syringe availability in local pharmacies in different areas of a city, then a random selection of city pharmacists may be invited to participate in the focus group. One thing to remember, however, is that if you want 8–12 group participants, it is probably a good idea to invite 18–20 because every possible participant will not be able to attend the group. Therefore, it might be a good idea to have group members RSVP if they plan to attend, and the facilitator can plan for either one group or two, depending on the number of interested participants. Capturing a representative sample of group participants is very important because you want the views of the group to be as close to the overall population as possible. One way that a sample may be biased, for example, is that if the needs assessment team wanted to capture the view of pharmacists on OTC syringe purchases and only invited pharmacists from the upper-middle class areas of town. Pharmacists in this area may have a very different view on OTC syringe purchases compared to pharmacists who work in areas where drug use is a significant problem and clientele often "scam" pharmacists to get syringes to inject drugs. Another option might be to have multiple focus groups if time and resources permit; this would result in as many opinions as possible.

Other considerations for the focus group participant selection should include the demographics of the population you want to represent. For example, are there particular ethnic or minority groups that should be represented—and how? It may be necessary to recruit more of these individuals to ensure that your focus group represents your target population.

Age is another consideration—do you need an open range of participants or do you want to target a more homogenous group (such as only individuals over age 50 years or only individuals between the ages of 22 and 25 years)? Other considerations may include a professional affiliation or particular amount of experience working with a particular population or in a particular agency. Each of these questions address the importance of recognizing important characteristics of the target population that you want to represent in your focus group.

Following decisions about the charge/mission/problem to explore, the size of the group, and the participants to invite, the needs assessment team conducting a focus group must also decide on specific open-ended questions to present to the group. Focus group questions need to be constructed in an open-ended manner to permit a great deal of discussion. Examples of good focus group questions include:

- How would you describe the most effective programs offered by this agency?
- What service or program is the agency missing?
- If you were the agency director, how would you improve the agency?

Each of these questions should generate useful discussion for the needs assessment.

Examples of questions that should not be used in a focus group include those in this format:

- Do you enjoy the programming offered by this agency?
- How much time do you spend on program homework?
- Do you have a good relationship with your counselor?

None of these questions allow the participants to elaborate or discuss the topic. Findings generated from these questions will likely not be very informative for the needs assessment project. When designing your focus group questions, avoid questions that can be answered with a "yes," "no," or other short-answer response. We recommend about 8–10 questions for a 1-hour group. It is also suggested that a good question to add at the end is "Is there anything else that we should have asked?" This may allow participants who have been thinking about something stimulated by past questions to respond and also provides a nice closure.

Once the questions are selected, the next step is to decide on the setting for the group. The needs assessment team should be sure that the venue is in a location that is close for all of the participants to travel, that it is a comfortable space large enough to accommodate all the participants, and that it provides a quiet and confidential area for the group. In addition, the venue should be accommodating to all participants (i.e., it should include handicap accessibility), be easy to find with directions, and have plenty of free parking. The goal is to make travel to and participation in the focus group as easy as possible for group participants. If financial resources permit, then you may also want to consider a small monetary incentive or travel reimbursement for participants. If possible, light refreshments are also recommended because they allow for social time that can place group members at ease when the group begins.

The needs assessment team should spend some time with the group facilitator before the session to be sure that he/she understands each of the questions and the overall purpose of the group. The group facilitator may also review some "ground rules" for the session, which may include respecting others opinions, allowing one person to talk at a time, and encouraging everyone to respond openly because there are no right or wrong answers. In addition—particularly if you are working with a client population—the facilitator may want to review any safety concerns related to the participants' confidentiality. Productive and informative focus groups are typically those where the facilitator is able to keep the participants on task, the group members feel that they can respond freely, and questions are asked without suggesting a desired response. To capture as much information as possible, we recommend audio-taping the sessions and transcribing the notes after the group. If audio-taping is too intrusive or not comfortable for the participant population, then it is recommended that at least one and preferably two research assistants accompany the facilitator to record all the participant responses. If notes are taken, then it is also recommended that they be transcribed as soon as possible after the group so the discussion is fresh in the research assistant's memory.

The final step in the focus group process is to analyze the findings and prepare the report (more about analyzing qualitative data—such as transcripts from focus groups—will be covered in Chapter 4). The primary point to consider in analyzing findings and preparing the report is to not lose sight of the needs assessment question. Primary and secondary themes will emerge as a result of the focus group discussion that may at times present interesting findings not directly related to the overall purpose of the needs assessment. It is possible to get distracted. Keep in mind that the goal is to use the focus group data to illuminate an issue or concern so that a response to the needs assessment question can be implemented by the agency or community.

Community Forums

Considering the rich and valuable data that can be obtained from focus groups, a needs assessment team might be tempted to try a similar approach where individuals from the community could be invited to attend a community forum. Community forums are public meetings or hearings where members of a community state their preferences or present their demands. Although this can be an informative way of gathering observational data in a very inexpensive and time-efficient manner, a word of caution for the needs assessment researcher: these meetings can sometimes be a forum to air complaints or disagreements with a current system or process. A small minority of individuals can dominate the meeting and place the agency on the defensive. In these cases, the meetings can be loud, boisterous, and poorly attended. For the most part, clients typically seen by social workers or treatment providers who may have valuable insight into a particular problem seldom attend such meetings. In contrast to focus groups, the needs assessment team will have much less control of the meeting or the topics that arise. Still, if the needs assessment team can create an interest in the community for a needs assessment forum and if good representation of individuals from the community attend, then this approach to needs assessment may yield some valuable information. However, the weakness of this approach is that those who attend and express their views may not be representative of the community or its needs.

Table 3.1 Advantages and Disadvantages to Focus Groups and Community Forums

Advantages:
- Both can inexpensively yield a significant amount of data in a short amount of time.
- There is an opportunity to capture perspectives of a number of clients at one time.
- There is minimal risk or harm to clients.
- Minimal expertise is needed by the research team.

Disadvantages:
- Views expressed in the group may not represent the entire population of respondents.
- Responses may be limited by the questions that are asked or responses by dominant speakers.
- Participants may be selected based on criteria rather than a random sample of the whole population

Unobtrusive Measures

Needs assessment designs can be inexpensive, require little staff time, and limited expertise when using unobtrusive measures. Unobtrusive measures are those that do not involve direct interaction with human participants (Berg, 1998). The interest in unobtrusive measures among social science researchers is that these approaches allow a researcher to access information in different areas and settings without introducing the "artificial" environment or stimulus that may come from the presence of a researcher. Examples of unobtrusive measures collected in social science research include public records (number of suicides, number of children receiving free school lunches, number DUI arrests, and number of substantiated cases of child abuse) as well as private archives of documents such as autobiographies, journals, and diaries (Berg, 1998).

Similar to social science researchers, needs assessment researchers can also gather important and meaningful data using unobtrusive measures. For example, *rates under treatment* is a type of needs assessment that relies on existing agency data (Royse, 2004). In this type of design, a needs assessment researcher would examine the profiles of an agency's clients from its management information systems (MIS), quarterly reports, or review of client files. Data generated from this approach could then be compared to census information for the larger population. This type of comparison can reveal which groups are being over- or underserved, and perhaps identify specific problems that may not be currently addressed by the agency. For example, a review of clients who have dropped out of service might, on inspection of client records, result from lack of evening hours, child care, or transportation. If enough clients are being lost because of one of these problems, then it is possible that the agency could investigate reallocating resources to address the documented need.

Agency data can also provide information about trends, perhaps indicating that a problem in the community is getting worse. For example, if agency records are examined for a 3-year period and the needs assessment team finds that the rates of depression among a population of pregnant mothers has increased over the past 2 years, then these findings can be addressed by the agency. However, these findings could mean that either the problem is truly increasing or the agency has somehow been successful in its outreach to pregnant women and, subsequently, has obtained more of these admissions with mental health issues. Either way, these trends are the basis for discussion and possibly warrant further investigation.

Secondary Data Collection

Searching agency level data is one example of an unobtrusive approach to information gathering known as secondary data collection. By definition, secondary data analysis involves the analysis of an existing data set that results in knowledge, interpretations, and conclusions. Secondary data collection can include a range of data sources from agency level records (e.g., number of clients with a dual diagnosis) to municipal police data, county records (number of DUI cases in local circuit court), state records (number of fatal accidents on state highways), or national data sets (national census data). Secondary data sources abound (e.g., school dropouts, health department cases of tuberculosis, sexually transmitted diseases, etc.) and are often public record (absent, of course, personally identifying information). There is usually no cost, or it is nominal. Exploring what might be available in the way of day from established agencies or authorities is often a very smart move for those wishing to conduct a needs assessment in their community.

Although data collection from agency files is an excellent way to document needs of a particular group, another method of secondary data collection that may be very useful for a needs assessment team is the analysis of existing state and/or national databases. Here is an example: A researcher at the local university has been given a small grant to examine the treatment needs of patients who are HIV-positive in a regional area. During the planning stages of the needs assessment, the researcher decided that it would be important to understand the HIV seropositivity among residents of the target area relative to a national comparison. In other words, she wanted to examine how the trends in HIV-positive status looked for males compared to females, for African-Americans compared to Caucasians, and for older vs. younger county residents. In addition, she was also interested in looking at the most common means of contracting HIV, including heterosexual contact, homosexual contact, and injection drug use.

The first step in her needs assessment included secondary data collection from the Centers for Disease Control HIV/AIDS Surveillance Report (http://www.cdc.gov/hiv/topics/surveillance/resources/reports/index.htm). The HIV/AIDS Surveillance Report includes information about AIDS and HIV case reports in the United States and is also presented by state and metropolitan statistical area. In addition to the *incidence* rates (newly reported cases of HIV in the area), the report also includes methods of exposure to the HIV virus, gender comparisons, race/ethnicity comparison, and *prevalence* (existing cases) by age group. This series of reports allows the researcher to access important information about HIV cases in her area and helps to generate the first step in her needs assessment project (additional information about analyzing secondary data is presented in Chapter 4).

Internet Options

Over the past few years, the Internet has grown in popularity and in utilization for both personal and professional use. The Internet is another example of an unobtrusive approach that can yield valuable secondary data for a needs assessment project. Most private and public agencies have local access to the Internet, making it an easy and convenient way to gather data. The following table (Table 3.2) presents some commonly used sites for needs assessment projects. This list is certainly not exhaustive and others may be found using active Internet search engines (such as Google www. google.com, Yahoo www.yahoo.com, AltaVista www.altavista.com, and Ask.com www.ask.com) and typing in key words associated with the needs assessment project to identify other possible state or national data sources.

Table 3.2 Internet Resources for Needs Assessment Projects

National Center for Health Statistics (http://www.cdc. gov/nchswww/default.htm)	This site's links lead to information such as descriptions of recent health surveys and data collections on vital statistics. This link was developed and managed by the Centers for Disease Control and Prevention.
Bureau of Labor Statistics (http://stats.bls.gov/)	The Bureau of Labor Statistics, updated by the Department of Labor, provides FTP links for downloading raw data on Local Area Unemployment Statistics and Geographical Profiles.
County and City Data Books (http://fisher.lib.Virginia .EDU/ccdb/)	Search settings allow you to select from a list of variables (population, housing, education, income, etc.) for U. S. cities and counties for years 1988 and 1994. Not a scholarly focus, but a quick guide for comparison of data trends.
FedStats (http://www.fedstats.gov/)	This site includes a listing for approximately 70 federal agencies (e.g., National Center for Health Statistics) with links to information on statistics, databases, etc. The site is maintained by the Federal Interagency Council on Statistical Policy.
U. S. Census Bureau (http://www.census.gov/)	Start with the button "Get State Profile!" (select a state); a state map displays; click on the county to find census-related information specific to that location. Provided by the U.S. Census Bureau.
White House Briefing Rooms (http://www .whitehouse.gov/news/fsbr .html)	Latest federal statistics may be accessed through three links from the opening page: Economics Statistics Briefing Rooms; Social Statistics Briefing Rooms; and FedStats (described above). Some data overlaps with the Census Bureau and other government agency reports, but this site might be easier to use.
Cancer Control P.L.A.N.E.T. (http://cancercontrolplanet .cancer.gov/)	This site provides access to data and resources that can help planners, program staff, and researchers to design, implement and evaluate evidence-based cancer control programs.

Source: http://library.downstate.edu/commsite/datalink.html

Geographic Information Systems and Needs Assessment

An additional unobtrusive approach that can be useful for needs assessment teams is mapping. The rapid development of Geographic Information Systems (GIS) and related mapping software can provide valuable perspectives for the needs assessment team. There are two prime ways GIS data can be employed in a needs assessment effort. First, GIS allows needs assessment researchers to map where clients live. The needs assessment team can create maps that indicate areas of the city or community where there may be disparities in service use resulting from age, geography, income levels, or race/ethnicity. Using data from agency records (e.g., zip codes), maps can be created locating areas dense with client residences. Overlay maps can also be created that rely on other sources (e.g., Census data) so that the needs assessment team can determine if there are pockets of population in the community from which few clients originate. (This might suggest the need for a public relations campaign to let individuals living in those areas know about available services. However, the mapping technique might also reveal that the agency needs to create a branch or satellite office to reach out to portions of the community where there are few clients. Agency data could be used to locate clients who have had the poorest outcomes in the program or to identify where referrals in the area are coming from).

Second, GIS approaches allow the needs assessment team to map existing social service resources. Locating the community's service inventory on a single map can show, as in the aforementioned example, whether there are areas in the community where services are not located or where key facilities (e.g., hospitals, shelters) are situated relative to key transportation routes. GIS can also be used to estimate distances and drive times. For additional reading on GIS mapping, see Hillier (2007).

Pros and Cons of Unobtrusive/Secondary Data Sources

Although secondary data collection from a variety of sources (including local, state, national data sources, the Internet, and GIS approaches) can provide valuable data for a needs assessment project, there are limitations to these approaches. Depending on the data needed for the needs assessment project, the team must be aware of the source of the data. For example, if the team is interested in included estimates on the number of drug-exposed children in a state's child welfare system, then they should not rely on data from one agency to project those numbers. In addition, it can be difficult to access data in a useable format from some datasets. Limitations may include the omission of certain key variables that would provide key information needed for the project (such as the street, block, or county level identifiers) or the need for a particular software package to analyze the data. To create databases, some agencies may have hired programmers for that sole purpose, and occasionally one encounters difficulty in downloading or even gaining access to these databases because of their uniqueness. That is, the needs assessor could be limited to paper copies of reports or tables already prepared for some other purpose. Needs assessment teams using secondary data must always be aware of the limitations of using secondary data because the data is not collected by the team and may not have been collected with a similar vision or purpose in mind for using the data. Still, there are decided benefits to examining data that may already exist in the community or in an electronic database.

Using an unobtrusive data collection approach has some definite advantages for a needs assessment team with regard to time, money, and expertise. However, there are also some disadvantages. Examples of advantages and disadvantages to using unobtrusive data collection approaches are presented in Table 3.3.

Survey Approaches

So far, we have discussed needs assessment designs that can be used with limited time, money, and expertise for a particular project. However, there are other approaches that can be used if the needs assessment researcher has a little more time, money, and expertise. Possibly the most popular form of needs assessment involves some sort of community survey. Generally, surveys can be thought of as snapshots of attitudes, beliefs,

Table 3.3 Advantages and Disadvantages to Unobtrusive Data Collection

Advantages to unobtrusive data collection approaches include:
- Data are already collected, saving considerable time and effort
- Any bias associated with data collection can be known
- No risk or harm to clients, particularly if data is not identified by client
- Can examine changes in social problems over time
- Inexpensive

Disadvantages include:
- Historical records of interest may not be available because of lost or damaged files
- Changes in data collection strategies over time
- Data collection may not be required or done consistently across data collectors
- Recent data may be limited by a lag in reporting
- Incompatibility of software, databases for ease of manipulation
- Internet data may not be from a credible source

or behaviors at one point in time for a particular group of respondents. Surveys are valuable tools for social workers conducting needs assessment projects because they offer the best opportunity to uncover special needs within their communities or within populations of clients. Surveys provide information about what the targeted population knows or perceives about the availability and accessibility of services and can also identify unmet needs or gaps in services. These surveys can range in complexity from the "home-grown" type designed by the needs assessment team to those that use already validated survey measures, to those based on rigorously selected samples that provide generalizability of the findings. Again, the selection of a survey needs assessment design—whether a small targeted survey or a large probability survey—largely depends on the availability of resources and the scope of the project.

Before moving into a more specific discussion of types of surveys that can be used in needs assessment projects, it is important to review some key terms related to survey data collection that may be helpful:

- *Generalizability* – the extent to which survey findings represent the views of the larger population; largely affected by the sampling approach

- *Population* – the entire group that survey findings are expected to represent
- *Sample frame* – a selected group (or subset) from the larger population from which the target sample will be randomly selected
- *Sample* – a selected group (or subset) from the larger population
- *Sampling approach* – the way that a sample is chosen from a larger population
- *Sampling bias* – a possible problem that can occur when the sample is not representative of the larger population due to some characteristic of the sampling approach

To put these terms into context, consider Example 1:

A survey of holiday shoppers is conducted by a retail firm in Dallas, Texas to determine the most popular gift ideas the day after Thanksgiving. The firm sends one data collector to a mall in Dallas. The data collector stands in front of a popular music store all day and attempts to interview those going into the store. At the end of the day, he has 50 surveys completed.

Now, consider Example 2:

A survey of holiday shoppers is conducted by a retail firm in Dallas, Texas to determine the most popular gift ideas the day after Thanksgiving. The firm sends 50 data collectors to one mall in each of the 50 states. The data collectors were instructed to arrive at the mall when stores opened at 6:00 a.m. and to change their position at least every 30 minutes to capture people in different areas of the mall. At the end of the day, each data collector was expected to have 100 surveys completed—for a total nationwide sample of 5,000.

In each of these examples, you can see that the sampling approach has a major impact on the interpretation of survey findings when the study is completed. In Example 1, the data will very likely describe the most popular gift ideas of music shoppers in Dallas, Texas. We might expect these shoppers to be younger and, besides music, interested in video games and small electronics. In Example 2, the larger sample is more likely to cover a broader spectrum of shoppers and to better represent the average American shopper the day after Thanksgiving. In addition, because the data collectors were instructed to move around to different parts of the mall, they likely captured shoppers interested in different types of gifts, which increases the generalizability of survey findings.

It should also be noted in each example that the commitment of the research firm—both in terms of financial resources and staff time—is considerably different. See a hypothetical budget in Table 3.4.

As you can see, the amount of resources required for a needs assessment project can be a primary consideration. The needs assessment team has to weigh the amount of information that is attainable by the amount of funds available and the staff time that can be devoted to the project. The following sections present more information about small targeted surveys and large probability surveys to help you make this decision.

Small Targeted Surveys

Small targeted surveys are typically conducted with a small group of people who are easily available to the needs assessment team. Although they may be believed to be representative of the target population, there is no good way with small samples to know how well they resemble the population.

Table 3.4 Needs Assessment Hypothetical Budget

Example 1		Example 2	
1 Data collector salary 1 day	$500	50 Data collector salaries 1 day	$25,000
Local travel	$25	Airfare and national travel	$10,000
Data entry and analysis 50 surveys	$100	Data entry and analysis 5000 surveys	$10,000
Total	$625		$45,000

Small survey samples are often samples of convenience. A sample of convenience is one that can be drawn quickly and easily and is typically an existing group of people (such as a class of students enrolled in a social work research class at a local university).

Small targeted surveys involve collecting information from a small group within a larger group or community, without trying to use them for overall representation of the larger population (Hampton & Vilela, 2007). One possible limitation with these surveys is that you may need to conduct several rounds of data collection (e.g., several small samples) to get a good picture of how the larger population may respond. The goal of a small targeted survey is to mirror results that you would have gotten with a larger group without the time and burden of rigorous sampling (Hampton & Vilela, 2007). For example, let's say you want to know what percentage of people in your county would make use of a weight loss program. Getting every resident in a county with 25,000 people to fill out a survey would be a huge task. Instead, you decide to survey a sample of 50 people at the local Walmart and find out how they feel about the program, the number of people they think might attend, and the number of people they know who are in need of a weight loss program.

Small targeted surveys are not limited to a focus on consumers and may also be administered to organizations and treatment providers. One example of this survey approach may be a social work professor who was awarded a small grant to design and implement training for mental health practitioners on evidence-based practices for co-occurring mental health and substance abuse disorders. To implement the study, the professor needed to know which mental health agencies in the state provided services to clients with co-occurring disorders, the current state of evidenced-based practices in those agencies, the types of interventions that were currently being used, and the willingness of agencies and treatment providers to participate in the study. She decided to conduct a needs assessment to answer these questions and developed a short survey for community mental health agency directors in her state. She included a number of questions to capture information on the types of services provided, and she also included a standardized scale on organizational readiness to adopt and implement evidence-based practices. By including both types of measures and randomly selecting a small, representative group of 30 agency directors in the state, she was able to gather some very important and meaningful data for her project.

Another example of a small targeted survey is with key informants who are likely to know about the needs of a community as a result of their positions. These individuals may be treatment providers, physicians, social service workers, clergy, lawyers and judges, and so on. This type of key informant survey was recently used in a study to determine the prevalence of prescription drug use in a small area of Appalachia (Staton-Tindall, Havens, Leukefeld, & Burnette, 2007). Surveys were administered to key informants in health, mental health, education, law enforcement agencies, as well as other identified community business leaders. Findings from the study indicated not only that prescription drug use was a major problem in the area but that perspectives on how drugs were obtained and availability of treatment opportunities varied widely, depending on the key informant respondent.

Large Probability Surveys

Small targeted surveys are useful tools to gain information when there is limited time, limited resources, and limited expertise. However, if the needs assessment team has a bit more time, resources, and expertise, then a larger probability survey would provide a more rigorous and scientifically valid design for the needs assessment project if the question warrants. The primary distinction between this type of survey and the smaller targeted survey involves a more detailed sampling process and more resources for data collection. A probability sampling method utilizes a random selection of survey participants from a larger group or population. The basic definition of random selection is that each person in the population under study has an equal chance of being selected to participate in the survey. A major advantage to being able to use a probability sample compared to a convenience sample is that each person within a population or sampling frame has the opportunity to be selected for the study, which significantly increases the generalizability of study findings to the larger population.

There are numerous Internet sources that can provide assistance in determining how many people need to complete survey data to get results that are representative of the target population (for examples, see Creative Research Systems www.surveysystem/sscalc.htm and Raosoft www.raosoft.com/samplesize.html). These sites are very helpful in selecting a sample size because they allow you to consider *margin of error* (the amount of error that you can tolerate) and the *confidence level* (the amount of uncertainty you can tolerate).

Table 3.5 presents some examples of random sampling strategies for a large probability survey of university college students to better understand resources needed to enhance health and mental health services on campus.

As you can see, there are numerous ways to capture a scientifically rigorous survey sample for your needs assessment project. The consideration again comes down to the resources available to you and the scope of your project. An additional factor that comes into play with a large probability survey is level of expertise. Ensuring that the sampling strategy is a valid and reliable approach to achieving representativeness of your sample (to the larger population) is an important undertaking. It requires a significant amount of planning, time, and resources. Because we are also likely talking about larger sample sizes, the data entry, analysis, and interpretation of study findings are also more labor-intensive. The end product will not only provide valuable information for your needs assessment project but may also lend itself to scientific writing for professional journals or national conferences.

Survey Method Modality

Although the appropriate sampling strategy is a key consideration in probability surveys, the survey method modality is also important. The primary methods of survey data collection include:

- Mailed surveys
- E-mail or Web-based surveys
- Telephone surveys
- Personal interviews

Table 3.5 Sampling Strategies for Needs Assessment Projects

Sampling strategy	Definition	Example
Simple random sampling	Each individual in the target population has an equal chance of being chosen	Sample of 1,000 students drawn from all students on a university enrollment list.
Systemic sampling	Each individual in the target population has a chance of being chosen, but only a certain fixed number of participants will be chosen	Target sample of 100 students, selected as every 10th student on an enrollment list after deciding a random starting place.
Stratified random sampling	Each individual in a particular group has a chance of being selected, but selected proportionate to that group's representation in the larger population	Separate sample frames are created for Caucasian and African-American students, and then a sample is selected including 65% Caucasian and 45% African-American, which is representative of the overall university student population
Cluster sampling	Each individual in a naturally occurring group or cluster has a chance of being selected	Separate all southeastern university campuses into clusters by state, randomly sample the clusters, and survey all the college students in each state that is surveyed

Each survey approach offers unique advantages and disadvantages—many of which relate to time, resources, and expertise. Table 3.6 presents examples of the possible requirements of time, resources, and expertise involved in each method.

The mailed survey requires the least amount of time, resources, and expertise to get into the field, plus it has the added advantage of allowing a significant amount of data collection to occur at one time. However, a disadvantage of a mailed survey is that the needs assessment team may have little control over response rates, which if they are low, introduce a potential concern for sampling bias. E-mail or Internet-based surveys

Table 3.6 Requirements of Needs Assessment Survey Approaches

Survey approach	Time	Resources	Expertise
Mailed survey	Low for design	Low, as long as surveys are hand processed	Medium for instrument design and data analysis
E-mail survey	Medium for design	Medium for data management	Medium for design and data analysis
Telephone survey	Medium for calls and staff training	Medium to high for number of staff to make calls	Medium for data analysis and instrument design
Personal interviews	High for scheduling, conducting interviews	High for number of staff, travel, and time commitment	High for training staff, data collection, and data analysis

Source: Simons-Morton, Greene, & Gottlieb, 1995

and telephone surveys take a little more time in designing the interview or questionnaire. Of course, calling people to get a live voice on the phone is very labor-intensive. Despite best efforts, response rates may be a potential problem because of such factors as telephone answering machines. However, by comparison, the needs assessment team can call and schedule potential respondents for a personal interview. The interview allows for the most complex and thorough questioning of respondents, yet the trade off is the amount of time required for scheduling and conducting interviews, as well as the amount of training for staff to collect, enter, and analyze data. The "best approach" for the needs assessment depends on the primary questions you want answered and the resources available to the project.

Designing Valid Questions

To design valid questions for your survey, the first decision that you must consider is: What data must be collected? This relates back, you will remember, to the first point of this chapter, which was to understand the scope of work that your needs assessment project must address. More specifically, you have to consider the specific content areas where information is needed. Once you have given a great deal of thought to the time, resources, and expertise that your project will demand and chosen the survey approach you will use, the next step is the construction of the actual questions to include in the needs assessment. Your options include open-ended questions and closed-ended questions. *Open-ended questions* allow the respondents to think about the question and generate a response without a predetermined response set. An example of an open-ended question is, "What are the most commonly requested services at intake interviews for this agency?" Although open-ended questions often allow the maximum freedom for participants to craft a response to questions, this question structure creates a time-consuming task for data entry and analysis (we will further discuss qualitative data coding in Chapter 4). On the other hand, *closed-ended* questions with predetermined response rates such as "Agree" or "Disagree" may seem a bit more limited in the amount of data that are generated, but they are much easier to enter into a database and analyze. An example of a closed-ended question with well-defined response categories follows:

> I find the services at this agency to be a good fit for my health-care needs.
> 1 – Strongly disagree
> 2 – Disagree
> 3 – Neutral
> 4 – Agree
> 5 – Strongly agree

The decision to use open- or closed-ended responses may be influenced by the survey modality that the needs assessment team is planning to use. For example, in mail surveys, respondents can take a look at all of the response categories before choosing an option. However, in telephone surveys, it may be very difficult to keep the question and the responses in mind when trying to make a decision. Consider the aforementioned example—can you imagine being the survey respondent on the other end of a telephone and being asked to remember all five of those choices and the question they are supposed to address?

Another consideration is that in a mailed survey, you can go back and respond to items that were difficult the first time. In a telephone survey, items should be worded so that they make sense to the participant because it may not be possible to repeat parts of the survey. Other important considerations for mail and E-mail/Internet surveys include clear readability of the instrument. In comparison to telephone surveys or personal interviews, the mail or E-mail survey respondent will not have the chance to ask questions if they do not understand, which may increase the risk that they will just pick a response or leave it blank—both of which can compromise the data.

Across each modality, questions should be designed with respect for differences that can arise from cultural factors, social economic status, and even gender. For example, persons with low levels of education may not respond to written surveys to the same extent as persons with more education. Persons who are not native English speakers may be more hesitant to provide sensitive information than those who were born in this country. Furthermore, surveys of non-English speakers must, of course, be translated into the desired language and then back-translated to make sure of the accuracy of the translation. When designing questions for your needs assessment, you must always consider the nature of the content, the intended survey approach, and the targeted respondents. It is a good idea to involve ethnically diverse individuals in planning your study or at least reviewing questionnaires and so forth if minority groups are going to be targeted in your needs assessment. Finally, pilot-test your instruments to ensure that they are culturally sensitive and contain no bias.

In writing questions for your data collection instrument, there are numerous "pitfalls" that you must avoid in the development of your survey items. Table 3.7 outlines some common mistakes in designing survey questions that can sabotage the usefulness of your survey data.

Designing valid questions for your needs assessment is an important process. The most important considerations are: What data do you want

Table 3.7 Common Mistakes in Designing Survey Questions

Problem	Example	Solution
Double-barreled questions	Have you exercised regularly or eaten pizza in the past 30 days?	Make this two questions: 1) Have you exercised regularly in the past 30 days? 2) Have you eaten pizza in the past 30 days?
Leading questions	Aren't you a supporter of the recent smoking ban in public restaurants?	How much do you support the recent restaurant smoking ban? 0 – Not at all 1 – Somewhat 2 – A great deal
Unavailable information	How many clients in this agency were registered as Independents in the 1992 presidential election?	How many clients served by this agency have registered to vote?
Use of technical terms	Would this agency benefit from enhanced training on evidence-based practices on EMDR?	What therapy approaches used in this agency are supported by research?
Insensitive language	How do you right-wingers feel about gay marriage?	How do you feel about same gender marriages?
Inflammatory terms	Are you a "problem drinker"?	How many alcoholic drinks do you typically consume in one week?
Non-mutually exclusive choices	How many clients a week reschedule their appointments? 1) 1 – 10 2) 10 – 20 3) Almost all	How many clients a week reschedule their appointments? 1) 1 – 10 2) 11 – 20 3) More than 20
Vague or ambiguous terms	How many times in your lifetime have you seen a doctor?	How many times in the past year have you visited your physician?
All-inclusive terms	Do you always eat breakfast?	On average, how many days a week do you eat something for breakfast? 1) 1 – 3 2) 4 – 5 3) 6 – 7
Negatively constructed items	Do you agree that it is wrong for people to not go to church?	How important is church attendance to you? 1) Not at all 2) Somewhat 3) Considerably 4) Extremely

Source: Royse, 2004

to collect? and What type of survey modality will you be using? After that, decisions around designing questions are the creative and fun part of the planning process. In fact, the needs assessment team may also want to include the agency stakeholders or others vested in the needs assessment project to review the instrument prior to distribution for additional feedback and to input ideas. The team may also want to pilot-test the questions with a small group to be sure that all the questions make sense, that pitfalls mentioned earlier have been successfully avoided, and response options are clear.

Evaluating Standardized Instruments

An alternative to developing your own questions for your needs assessment data collection tool is to use standard instruments that are already available. These existing instruments may present a time savings because development of survey items can be very time-consuming. In addition, if the instrument or scale (short set of related items) has been used before, then important psychometric information such as reliability and validity are likely available, as well as possibly data for comparison to your sample.

Reliability refers to the dependability of an instrument—its ability to consistently reproduce (all things being equal) similar findings when it has been previously used. In other words, a reliable instrument increases the likelihood that a needs assessment researcher will get the same findings using this scale if she administers the survey again? One example of reliability is to have two independent researchers collect needs assessment data from agency files using a standardized code sheet. If one researcher identifies 64 client referrals from therapists in individual sessions with clients and the other researcher counts only 32 referrals from the same data, then the data collection procedure would not have very high reliability. Standardized instruments typically have scores to interpret reliability (e.g., Chronbach's alpha), and those scores should suggest agreement at least 75% to 80% of the time (Royse, 2008).

On a separate note, indicators of validity are also important to consider in evaluating standardized instruments. *Instrument validity* is an indicator that your needs assessment survey instrument measures what it was intended to measure. Using the aforementioned example, let's say that a researcher hurriedly selects a standardized instrument from an Internet site that she thinks is intended to measure alcohol use among parents of children who enter treatment at their clinic (Parental Alcohol Use Survey). She incorporates the survey into her intake assessment. When she begins to analyze her data, the findings do not make sense with what she expected from her client population. She further explores the survey instrument in other research articles and learns that the scale is intended to be completed by adult clients (not appropriate for children or adolescents) about their own childhood experiences with alcohol use by their parents. Because the instrument was being used differently from the specific purpose for which it was designed, it did not produce valid data for determining the prevalence of alcohol use among caregivers in their client population.

One advantage to using standardized instruments that have been used in other needs assessment projects or other social science projects is that these indicators of reliability and validity have typically been established and should be located in any articles you find that reported use of the instrument. In contrast, you will not have reliability and validity information on items that you or your team develops unless you do the necessary work. So, during the survey planning process, consider use of standardized instruments, if ones relevant to your project can be found. An example of an existing instrument that has been used in other studies and called the Survey of Program Training Needs (Rowan-Szal, Greener, Joe, & Simpson, 2007) is included as an example in the Appendix. Please note this scale is copyrighted and should be used with permission from the authors at Texas Christian University (see www.ibr.tcu.edu).

Table 3.8 presents some tips to consider when evaluating standardized instruments for use in your needs assessment project.

Methodological Limitations

Each of the needs assessment designs presented in this chapter has advantages and disadvantages that have been discussed along the way.

Table 3.8 Evaluating Standardized Instruments

Practicality: Is the instrument:
- affordable? Is the scale copyrighted and does it require purchase?
- accessible? Is it easy to obtain without copyright issues?
- easily understood by needs assessment respondents?
- easy to administer over the phone or in person?
- easy to score or interpret?
- appropriate for the time constraints of the study?

Psychometrics: Does the instrument have:
- solid reliability (yield similar results each time it is used)?
- sensitivity to detect increments of improvements?
- validity (measures what it is intended to measure)?

Appropriate for the project: Does the instrument:
- have the ability to yield data to answer the needs assessment question?
- fit within the overall scope of work for the project?
- provide data that is meaningful for the final report?

As a result, needs assessment findings should be interpreted with caution and in the context of the study design. A potential mistake that can be made by a needs assessment team is to overgeneralize findings—that is, to go beyond the scope of the study that was actually implemented. A detailed description of this potential limitation will be presented in Chapter 5.

Summary

This chapter has provided an overview of basic needs assessment designs that may be used in your project. Decisions about needs assessment designs must be guided by the available resources to conduct the project and the scope of the question to be addressed by the needs assessment project. The needs assessment team must make these decisions with the understanding that the end product may be higher or lower on scientific rigor. Stated differently, investing more time, financial resources, and expertise may provide opportunities for the creation of needs assessment designs that offer greater protection against skeptics and "nay-sayers." Table 3.9 provides a summary of designs that may be applied to different

Table 3.9 Evaluating Needs Assessment Designs

Time frame	*Finances*	*Expertise*	*Possible design*
6 months to 1 year (or even longer) to complete a needs assessment	Financial support—grants or other significant funding in excess of $1500 to complete the needs assessment*	Expertise—needs assessment researchers are primarily research and/or evaluation staff with some experience in needs assessment*	• Probability surveys; personal interviews
3-6 months to complete a needs assessment	Some financial support—small grants or funding ($500–$1500) to complete the needs assessment	Some expertise—needs assessment researchers are primarily staff with some experience in research or evaluation	• Small targeted surveys
Less than 3 months to complete a needs assessment	Limited financial support—small grants or funding ($500 or less) to complete the needs assessment	Limited expertise—needs assessment researchers are primarily agency staff or students who have other commitments and limited research or statistical expertise	• Focus group • Community forum • Unobtrusive measures including secondary data collection from agency files

Resources ↓ — Scientific rigor ↓

*Note: In needs assessment projects that are funded by larger grants (e.g., $20,000 or more), data collection may be contracted by a professional polling organization. This could be a tremendous advantage for the needs assessment team in that they do not have to focus on the process of data collection but are able to work with a trusted source with expertise in the area.

needs assessment projects, depending on the available resources and scope of work:

The next consideration that the needs assessment researcher must focus on after choosing the needs assessment design is the data analysis approach. This will be the focus of Chapter 4, and will draw on many of the same decisions made in choosing the right needs assessment design.

4

Analyzing the Needs Assessment Data

Once the needs assessment data have been collected, it is necessary to identify patterns and main themes, to interpret, and to disseminate the findings. This chapter will discuss ways of examining quantitative data using univariate and bivariate analysis. Analysis of qualitative data will also be covered for those who have used focus groups or questionnaires that have employed open-ended questions.

Topics to be explained in this chapter will include:

- Quantitative data analysis including data editing and checking, frequencies, and univariate analyses as well as examination of variables two at a time.
- Qualitative data analysis including understanding and interpreting themes and patterns in the data and drawing conclusions.
- Quantitative and qualitative data examples in needs assessment projects.

Quantitative Data Analysis

Quantitative data analysis includes the organization, analysis, and interpretation of numeric or numerically coded data (Montcalm & Royse,

2002). The measurement of variables and data analysis are characteristics of quantitative research, and provide ways to *(1)* summarize characteristics of a particular group; *(2)* use characteristics of a sample to estimate characteristics of the larger population; and *(3)* examine patterns of relationships within a particular group (Weinbach & Grinnell, 1998). In other words, quantitative data analysis is a way of taking all the data that you have collected in your needs assessment project and organizing it in a meaningful way.

Consider this scenario: A needs assessment team working with a community mental health agency is interested in understanding the number of clients who reported symptoms of depression on their intake form. Examine the examples of data presentation in Tables 4.1 and 4.2. Which table presents more useful data? Assuming that that these four clients make up the total sample (which is unlikely given the usual caseload at a mental health agency), the presentation of data in Table 4.2 is much more useful for comprehending the extent of mental health symptoms among the clients being served. This table shows the importance of organization of information to make the data collected easier to comprehend and use.

Quantitative data analyses typically accompany data collection approaches that involve a large number of subjects and numerous variables often collected through surveys or interviews. For example, building on our discussion in Chapter 3, when you use surveys or close-ended interviews to collect data for your needs assessment project, you would likely end up with data that consists of numbers or choices in response to study questions. You also might access or use secondary national datasets that are easily downloaded from the Internet. These are perfect candidates for

Table 4.1   Example of Raw Data for Clients Reporting Mental Health Issues

	Trouble sleeping	Felt sad or blue	Loss of appetite	Loss of energy
Client A	Yes	No	Yes	No
Client B	No	Yes	No	Yes
Client C	Yes	Yes	Yes	No
Client D	No	No	Yes	No

Table 4.2 Example of Summary of Data on Clients Reporting Mental Health Issues

	Percent Reporting Symptom at Intake
Loss of energy	25%
Trouble sleeping	50%
Felt sad or blue	50%
Loss of appetite	75%
Any symptom	100%

a quantitative data analysis approach. Other data collection strategies that yield text or written responses to open-ended questions (such as focus groups or community forums) are best analyzed using a qualitative data analysis approach (discussed more in the next section).

Quantitative data analysis is a logical, systematic process that follows a series of steps. Each of these steps will be discussed in detail in relation to needs assessment in the next few sections. Typically, the steps are:

1. Data coding
2. Data cleaning and analysis preparation
3. Frequencies and univariate analysis
4. Examining relationships between two or more variables

Data Coding

The data that you capture in needs assessments is not always ready to be directly entered into the computer. For ease in data analysis, response categories are usually converted to numbers and this is called *coding the data*. For example, if you were entering information from 250 surveys into a computer data base to tabulate the data, you will find that it takes fewer keystrokes to let numeric codes represent responses as shown below than to type out "single," "married," "separated/divorced," "female," and so forth. These codes are relatively arbitrary—that is, it makes no difference whether you use "3" for "single" or for "separated/divorced." However, you do have to be consistent. Also, it usually makes sense to let

"0" reflect the absence of some trait—it is just easier to remember that rule than it is to always memorize a new code. When you create a number code for every item in your questionnaire or interview schedule, this is called creating a *codebook*. Statistical programs like SPSS require data to be coded for all but the most elementary operations. Once a codebook is created, it can be shared with other individuals who are helping with the data entry. Each new project usually requires its own codebook.

Variable	Attribute	Code
Marital Status	Single	1
	Married	2
	Separated/divorced	3
Gender	Female	1
	Male	2
U.S. veteran	Yes	1
	No	0
Disabled	Yes	1
	No	0

Data Cleaning and Analysis Preparation

Cleaning and editing the data is an important first step in the process of data analysis. Depending on the volume of cases that your data collection file contains, there are a couple of different ways to begin. If your data collection file has a few cases (25 or less) and has not been entered into a database such as Microsoft Excel (office.microsoft.com/en-us/excel/default.aspx) or SPSS (Statistical Package for the Social Sciences, www.spss.com), then your data analysis may involve simply counting the occurrence of certain variables and tallying the responses. If this is your analytic approach, then the first step in cleaning your data might be to closely examine each case summary to check for any data collection errors. For example, if you were interested in documenting the number of days that clients reported drinking in the past 30 days, then each case should have data entries between 0 and 30. If a data collection error is detected (let's say one case had an entry of 32), one possibility might be to go back to the agency file to check the data. If this is not possible because of record access or timing, then another possibility might be to exclude the case from the data file. However, you should make every effort to avoid eliminating cases when there are small sample sizes because of the risk for overgeneralizing possible findings.

When your data file has more entries and a database has been established, you might consider running a frequency distribution to check for data entry errors. A frequency distribution will show you all of the entered values for a particular variable and is typically organized numerically. So, using the earlier example (the number of days drinking out of the past 30 days), the frequency distribution would show the number of records for each value between 0 and 30 and could be easily examined for values out of the target range between 0 and 30. A printout of the frequencies for each variable should be generated and examined for errors. Sometimes it is necessary to go back to the original questionnaires or data to determine where the problem lies and correct the error in your dataset.

Another suggestion is to save your "cleaned" data file—either in hard copy or as a dataset—as a separate file that is clearly marked "clean." You want to be sure that any data analysis that is conducted for the needs assessment report is done using the cleaned data file. This is important because you want to be sure that your analyses are conducted on data that are free from the problems that you corrected. Also, you want to be sure that the raw data is preserved in case you want to use it again.

Frequencies and Univariate Analyses

Frequencies and univariate analysis can provide some of the most useful and meaningful data for your needs assessment project. A *frequency* is a count of the number of cases or characteristics of certain cases—such as the number of males and number of females for a "gender" variable. A frequency is an example of *univariate analysis*, or examining the characteristics of one variable at a time. Because the goal of any needs assessment project is often to determine the needs of clients, agencies, or organizations targeted by the study, frequencies and univariate analysis enable the needs assessment team to identify the prevalence of certain types of needs within the data collection design. An example of a frequency distribution for the variable "age of participants" in a college-based needs assessment project might look like this:

Table 4.3 Example of Frequency Distribution for Participant Age

Age of participant	Frequency (f)	Percentage (%)
18	45	13.7%
19	57	17.3%
20	54	16.4%
21	59	17.9%
22	43	13.1%
23	32	9.7%
24	21	6.4%
25	18	5.5%
	$n = 329$	100%

It is possible to run a frequency distribution for variables in Microsoft Excel, which, using the Frequency syntax, allows you to calculate how often a particular value appears within a range of values (http://office.microsoft.com/en-us/excel/default.aspx). One potential problem with Excel is that generating a frequency or other univariate analysis requires typing a syntax command for a range of numbers. For someone proficient in Excel, this is likely an easy step; however, others may find it frustrating. Another option is a statistical package called SPSS. SPSS is widely used as an analytic database for social sciences. SPSS can be purchased at most university bookstores or online at www.spss.com. The program offers a tutorial that demonstrates the "point-and-click" method, which some may find easier to use than the program commands in Excel. The following sections will outline the steps for frequencies and other forms of univariate analysis with boxes to guide you through running each type of analysis in SPSS.

Frequencies

A frequency distribution for a variable will tell you the range of response choices and the number of participants selecting each response for the variable. Frequencies should be run again following data cleaning to ensure all variables contain valid responses.

SPSS: Analyze → Descriptive statistics → Frequencies → Select the variable of interest

Mean

The mean is the numerical average of the values for a given response. Examining the mean for a variable before and after data cleaning can be very helpful to ensure that the mean is within an expected range to control for *outliers* (values in the data that represent extremes). For example, in a sample of healthy adults, the mean number of emergency room (ER) visits in the past year should be small—maybe one or two visits. If the mean in your dataset for this variable is 20, then there may be some data miscoded (e.g., 20 instead of 02), or there could actually be several cases with an exorbitant number of ER visits that cause the mean to be much higher. Another way to "cross-check" the presence of outliers in your data, and the potential impact of those outliers on the mean score, is to examine the standard deviation. The *standard deviation* tells you how far an average score in the distribution varies from the mean (Montcalm & Royse, 2002). When variables have values that are fairly close together and there is little variation, the standard deviation is small. When variables have values that are more spread out and there is a great deal of variation, the standard deviation will be larger.

Median

Computing the median is another way of getting a special type of average. The median is the value that falls in the middle of a range of responses.

In a normally distributed sample with valid responses ranging from 0 to 30, it is expected that the median value be somewhere around 15. The median also provides a nice cross-check in data cleaning. Unlike the mean, the median is not influenced by extreme scores (e.g., one respondent made 45 trips to the ER last year).

Mode

The mode is the value that is most commonly reported by respondents. Using the earlier example about ER visits, in a sample of healthy adults, let's say that 60% of the adults made no visits to the ER. In that situation, the most common response to the question about the number of ER visits in the past year would be "0." Therefore, the mode would be "0" for this dataset, although the mean would be higher (e.g., high-usage respondents, even if they were in the minority, will pull the mean in the direction of the higher scores).

SPSS: Analyze → Descriptive statistics → Descriptives

Under the "options" for descriptives, you can select mean, median, and mode.

Univariate analysis, including frequencies and measures of central tendency, are commonly used in needs assessment projects. Consider the following three examples and how the presentation of data, although somewhat simple, can still be helpful for service delivery and policy change.

In each of the examples provided, you can see how the presentation of basic frequencies to summarize the characteristics of the population is helpful in understanding the needs of the respondents included in the study. In each case, using the frequencies to present estimates of a particular need also translates readily to how that need might be addressed in setting priorities for services. In cases where funding is limited and resources have to be tailored to meet the needs of a population, using univariate analysis to determine the frequency of problems can then be organized in

> **Example 1: Health-Related Needs Following the September 11th Terrorist Attack**
> The New York City Department of Health and Mental Hygiene, in conjunc-
> tion with the Centers for Disease Control, conducted a community needs
> assessment in the months following the September 11, 2001 terrorist attack
> (Kramer, et al., 2002). The overall goal of the needs assessment was to iden-
> tify the health-related needs of New York City residents living in lower Man-
> hattan and the concerns of residents living near Ground Zero. The needs
> assessment team planned to use findings from the survey to set health-care
> priorities for the area, as well as to inform the development of public health
> interventions. Findings from the needs assessment project indicated that
> 66% of survey respondents reported nose or throat irritations, 50% re-
> ported eye irritation or infection, and 47% reported persistent coughing.
> Although the survey was completed a few months after the terrorist attack,
> most respondents (82%) reported that these health conditions continued to
> be a problem. In addition, although most people reported that they had ac-
> cess to health services (93%), some (14%) reported problems getting medi-
> cation prescriptions filled because of continuing problems with phone lines
> and transportation. With regard to mental health conditions, more than
> one-third (39%) reported symptoms of post-traumatic stress disorder that
> were above the screening cutoff, suggesting a need for additional mental
> health evaluation. In addition, 14% of respondents indicated that they used
> alcohol more than they used to prior to the attack, and 7% indicated that
> they likely needed to decrease their drinking. Survey findings were used to
> develop outreach efforts in lower Manhattan that focused on reducing ex-
> posure to harmful environmental toxins, managing psychological symptoms,
> and increasing availability of services. For more information, see www.cdc
> .gov/mmwr/preview/mmwrhtml/mm51SPa4.htm.

a hierarchical way. If an agency learns that 35% of their clients have mental health issues, 55% are involved in domestic violence situations, 25%
have substance abuse problems, and 15% have learning disabilities, then
resources could be structured so that domestic violence services are en-
hanced as a "first-tier" priority. Thus, quantitative data analysis that begins
with a series of univariate statistics, such as frequency distributions, can
be a valuable tool for a needs assessment team.

Example 2: Needs of Hurricane Katrina Survivors

The Centers for Disease Control, in conjunction with the Mississippi Department of Health, conducted a needs assessment to identify the public health needs with the goal of planning response efforts for victims of Hurricane Katrina (McNeil et al., 2006). Hurricane Katrina swept ashore on August 29, 2005 and has been estimated as the nation's most costly natural disaster in history. Hancock County, Mississippi was the state's most affected area. Needs assessment survey teams visited residents of the area within 3 weeks of the hurricane. Findings indicated that more than one-third (36%) of respondents reported that their homes were completely destroyed (also verified by the needs assessment team). Most respondents reported difficulty accessing basic needs, including water (26%), electricity (41%), indoor toilets (37%), and telephone services (53%). Health and mental health concerns were also reported. One-third of respondents (33%) reported having a family member who had sought medical care since the storm, about 34% said they had a family member who needed medical services at the time of the interview, and about 13% reported having a family member with mental health issues following the storm. Findings from this needs assessment were used to support the need for basic services to the area, including water and trash/debris removal as well as increasing access to health and mental health facilities in the area. For more information, see www.cdc.gov/mmwr/preview/mmwrhtml/mm5509a3.htm.

Examining Relationships Between Two or More Variables

Although analysis targeting one variable at a time can provide valuable data for your needs assessment project, sometimes your question requires you to examine relationships between two variables. One way to do this is with a crosstabulation, or crosstab. A *crosstab* analysis allows you to examine frequencies and percentages of values that are present for one variable from the perspective of another variable. For example, if you were interested in viewing the percent of students with failing grades for a class of fifth- and sixth-graders by gender, your crosstab might look like that in Table 4.4.

Table 4.4 Example of Analysis of Students Making Failing Grades in Windy Knoll
Elementary

	Fifth Graders	Sixth Graders
Males	14%	12%
Females	7%	9%

In this case, the percent of students making failing grades is consistently higher for male students than female students across the fifth and sixth grades.

SPSS: Analyze → Descriptive statistics → Crosstabs

Crosstabs not only allow you to see the frequencies and proportions of one variable in relation to another but also lends itself to testing for statistical significance. To say that a finding is *statistically significant* means that the likelihood of an event occurring by chance is less than your identified significance level (usually around 5%; for further discussion on statistical

---

Example 3: Mental Health Needs Among Homeless People

Salize et al. (2001) conducted a needs assessment to determine the prevalence of mental health disorders and mental health-care needs among a sample of homeless people. Findings indicated that the majority (69%) reported a current mental health disorder, and 82% reported lifetime prevalence of a mental health disorder. The needs assessment team found that both the lifetime and current prevalence of mental health disorders was greater among men than women, although their sample of women was significantly smaller than men (14 compared to 88). More than half of respondents in this study indicated that their mental health needs had not been addressed by formal treatment services (56%). An additional 40% indicated that their needs had been "partially" met by mental health services. Based on these findings, the needs assessment team recommended to the agency that more mental health outreach efforts be applied in the following ways: *(1)* serious psychiatric symptoms and co-occurring disorders; *(2)* physical health treatment combined with mental health services; and *(3)* rehabilitative services for basic needs.

significance, *see* Weinbach & Grinnell, 2007 or Montcalm & Royse, 2002). In other words, if you find that males fail more courses than the females and it is a significant difference between the two, then you can conclude that it is a real difference—unlikely to be a fluke or accident. In planning the needs assessment, your team should consider whether statistical tests may be required to address your needs assessment question.

Before we enter into a discussion of different types of analysis that you can conduct to determine statistical significance, it might be helpful to review some key terms that define levels of measurement for different types of variables. See Table 4.5 for a review of levels of measurement and examples.

Considering the aforementioned examples, you might decide that you need to perform statistical tests to answer the question of whether male and female clients of a local mental health agency differ on their intake scores for problem drinking. In this case, gender is the *independent variable* (variables that are expected to influence, affect, or cause changes in another variable), and the client's score on the problem-drinking index is the *dependent variable* (variable of interest being examined or explained). For a more detailed discussion on independent and dependent variables, *see* Royse (2008). You also might be interested in whether there are gender differences in the ratings of service satisfaction. Both of these questions might tell you a great deal about the services needed or quality of services provided at the agency.

Table 4.5 Definitions and Examples of Levels of Measurement

Level of measurement	Definition	Example
Nominal	Category	Gender is measured as either (1) male or (2) female
Interval	Numeric scores with equal intervals between values	Scores on an index of problem drinking where multiple items worth one point each sum to an overall at risk score
Ordinal	Categorical ranking	Rating of service satisfaction = (1) Poor (2) Fair (3) Good (4) Excellent

Table 4.6 Guidelines for Variable Types and Analysis

If your INDEPENDENT variable is …	If your DEPENDENT variable is …	Consider this test …
Nominal	Nominal	Chi-square
Nominal (2 groups)	Interval	t-test
Nominal (3 or more groups)	Interval	ANOVA
Interval	Interval	Correlation, Pearson's r

Source: Weinbach & Grinnell, 1998

Table 4.6 provides a quick reference guide for the types of analytic tests that you might perform based on the types of variables that you have in your dataset. There are many more statistical tests available, but four are commonly used in needs assessment projects.

If you have ordinal level measures, then they can typically be treated as nominal categories or occasionally as interval data and analyzed as noted earlier. A description of how to run each test in SPSS is provided below, as well as an example of how to present and interpret the findings.

Chi-Square

Chi-square is the statistical procedure that computes statistical significance (probability) based on the extent to which proportions of values within each of the cells in a crosstab differ from each other.

Table 4.7 Example of Chi-Square Analysis

Gender of participant	Ever treated for psychiatric problems		
	No	Yes	Total
Male	15 (50.0%)	15 (50.0%)	30 (100%)
Female	9 (45.0%)	11 (55.0%)	20 (100%)
Total	24 (48.0%)	26 (52.0%)	50 (100%)

Significance value of Pearson chi-square = 0.729

SPSS: Analyze → Descriptive statistics → Crosstab → Select the variables of interest placing the independent variable in the row bow and the dependent variable in the column box → Click the "statistics" button on the bottom left → check the "chi-square" box in the upper left corner

This chi-square analysis examines differences in history of psychiatric treatment between males and females at a mental health agency. If you look in the "yes" column for ever treated for psychiatric problems, then you can see that a slightly higher percentage of females (55%) than males (50%) reported a history of treatment. However, the statistical value of the chi-square statistic is 0.729, which is greater than 0.05, indicating that the proportions of treatment utilization do not differ significantly by gender in this analysis—that the differences between men and women are not statistically significant.

t-test and ANOVA

Statistical t-tests and analysis of variance (ANOVA) will be discussed together in this section because they are similar types of tests—both examine differences in means across groups. The t-test is used if you have only two groups of the independent variable, and the ANOVA is used if you have three or more groups of the independent variable.

Table 4.8 Example of a t-test Analysis

	Marital status	N	Mean	Standard Deviation	Standard Error Mean
Years of education	Single, never married	29	10.52	2.4	0.448
	Other marital status	21	11.95	1.9	0.411

Independent Samples t-test

	Test for equality of variances	F	Significance	t	df
Years of education	Equal variance assumed	5.311	0.26	−2.268	48

SPSS to run a *t*-test: Analyze → Compare Means → Independent samples *t*-test → Select the dependent measure as the test variable and the independent variable as the grouping variable (define levels based on values assigned to the different levels)

    SPSS to run an ANOVA: Analyze → Compare Means → One-way ANOVA → Select the dependent variable for the dependent variable box and select the independent variable for the factor box.

This *t*-test examines the number of years of education by participants in a needs assessment study who were single, compared to participants in an "other" marital status category. You can see that participants who were single reported slightly fewer years of education (10.52 years) than participants who reported another marital status (11.95). The second table gives you the significance value of 0.26, which is more than 0.05. Therefore, this finding is not considered statistically significant, meaning that we cannot be assured that the finding that single participants in this study had fewer years of education resulted from chance alone.

    This ANOVA examines the number of times that participants of different ethnic backgrounds in a needs assessment study reported being

Table 4.9 Example of ANOVA (**ANOVA**)

Descriptives - Number of Times Seriously Ill

	Marital status	N	Mean	Standard Deviation	Standard Error Mean
Race	Caucasian	24	4.42	3.2	0.654
	African-American	26	2.69	2.4	0.467
	Total	50			

ANOVA

	Sum of Squares	df	Mean Square	F	Sig.
Between groups	37.108	1	37.108	4.720	0.035
Within groups	377.372	48	7.862		
Total	414.480	49			

seriously ill. In the first table above, the means for Caucasian and African-American are circled. You can see that Caucasians reported being seriously ill 4.42 times compared to 2.69 times for African-Americans. Also, note that the significance value in the last column is 0.035—a value lower than 0.05, which indicates that this finding is statistically significant.

Correlations

Correlations examine the relationship between two interval level variables. The Pearson correlation coefficient is an indicator of the strength of the relationship, interpreted as the closer to 1.0 (or −1.0), the stronger the relationship. Any variable correlated with itself produces a correlation coefficient of 1.0. A positive correlation indicates that as values in one variable increase or decrease, so do values in the other variable. A negative correlation indicates that as values in one variable increase, values in the other variable decrease (and visa versa).

SPSS: Analyze → Correlate → Bivariate → select the two variables of interest

This correlation examines the relationship between the age of study participants and the number of times reporting being seriously ill. In

Table 4.10 Example of a Correlation Using Pearson's r

		Age of participant	Number of times seriously ill
Age of participant	Pearson correlation	1	0.603**
	Significance (two-tailed)		0.000
	n	50	50
Number of times seriously ill	Pearson correlation	0.603**	1
	Significance (two-tailed)	0.000	
	n	50	50

**Correlation is significant at the 0.01 level (two-tailed).

Table 4.10, the circled variable indicates that there is a significant relationship between the age of participants and the number of times being seriously ill. You can tell by looking at the positive value of the Pearson correlation value that this is a positive correlation, suggesting that as participant age increases, so does the number of times reporting being seriously ill.

The examination of two or more variables using statistical tests can provide some valuable data for a needs assessment project. An example of a needs assessment project where the team examined the relationship between two variables is presented below:

Example: Examining Relationships Between Two Variables in a Needs Assessment

In a separate needs assessment project, Acosta and Toro (2000) examined the community service utilization among homeless adults from Buffalo, New York. The needs assessment team was interested in utilization of a variety of community services among the homeless population, types of services that were needed, and difficulty experienced in obtaining needed services. Findings from this needs assessment indicated that the majority of the sample was male (74%), they were mostly persons of color (73%), more than half had no dependent children (55%), and about two-thirds had a substance abuse problem (74%). In examining service utilization in the past 6 months, 61% reported using homeless shelters and about half (48%) reported visiting a soup kitchen. The needs assessment team wanted to describe satisfaction with services in relation to the services that were utilized. They conducted a t-test to examine type of service utilization as the independent variable (soup kitchen/shelter vs. other types of services) and level of service satisfaction as the dependent variable (measures on a satisfaction scale). Findings indicated that homeless participants in this needs assessment study were significantly more satisfied with the services received in a soup kitchen compared to the shelter and other types of community services. Findings from this study suggest that there are a few targeted services in the community where outreach efforts to homeless populations might be needed. In addition, there may be a need for expanding the number of soup kitchens in the area.

Examining Multiple Variables at the Same Time

Another type of analysis that may be used in a needs assessment project is regression. Regression models allow you to examine a number of variables (both as a set and/or as individual variables) as predictors of some outcome variable. For example, an agency primarily serves substance abuse clients and defines a "positive treatment outcome" as abstinence at 6 months post-treatment discharge. As part of your needs assessment project, you may examine the factors that are most likely to predict abstinence in the client population—factors such as age (are clients who remain abstinent older or younger?); race (do African-Americans remain abstinent at similar rates as Hispanic clients?); gender (do males and females differ in rates of abstinence?); and so forth. Running regression models can be complicated and involve a detailed exploration of the data as an interim step. You want to be sure that variables are related to each other at the bivariate level before including them in a multivariate model. For more detail on regression analysis, see Weinbach and Grinnell (1998).

A specialized form of regression analysis is logistic regression, which is used when you want to predict an outcome variable that is categorical and has two levels (dichotomous). For example, if you were working in a county health department with indigent parents of newborns and emphasizing the importance of parents getting vaccinations for their babies, then a logistic regression could tell you which variable (age, gender, employment, number of children, education, etc.) was the best predictor of those parents who followed through and scheduled the recommended immunizations. Logistic regression models provide odds ratios for each predictor variable to inform you, based on statistical significance testing, how likely the predictor variable is to cause an effect on the outcome variable when other variables are considered in the same model. An example of a needs assessment project using logistic regression is included in the following box:

Example: Using Logistic Regression in a Needs Assessment Project

Beverly et al. (2005) conducted a community needs assessment to solicit community feedback to develop the educational and interdisciplinary health-care components of an aging initiative. The overall goal of the needs assessment was to influence state policy to improve health outcomes for the elderly through interdisciplinary clinical care and innovative educational programs. Their analysis included a series of univariate (frequencies) to profile the sample, including being mostly female (68%), mostly Caucasian (82%), between the ages of 65-84 (83%), and either married or widowed (84%). The team also conducted some bivariate analysis—in examining the relationship between race and health conditions. They found that non-Caucasian respondents were 1.6 times more likely to have diabetes, 1.6 times more likely to have memory problems, 1.3 times more likely to have high blood pressure, and 1.3 times more likely to have the flu than Caucasian elderly respondents. Findings from their study suggest that not only are health problems and the need for services high among the elderly, but there may be some racial/ethnic groups who are more at risk for certain health problems.

Qualitative Data Analysis

To this point, we have focused on data analysis techniques that involve the manipulation of numbers to answer questions for a needs assessment project. However, as we discussed in Chapter 3 some needs assessment data collection designs involve narrative as data in the form of open-ended interviews or focus group notes. This type of data requires a qualitative analytic approach. Qualitative data analysis involves taking words, phrases, or sections of text and coding data into constructs or categories. Those constructs can then be examined for themes or patterns that can describe the primary issues for the needs assessment project. Much like the initial cleaning with quantitative data, decisions about the qualitative approach can be made based on the volume of available data. For example, if your needs assessment team has hundreds of pages of notes from field observations, open-ended interviews, and agency record checks, then examining those notes for key themes might be difficult, and the needs assessment team might want to utilize computer software packages such as NVivo or Nud*ist (numerous computer packages exist and can be located using an Internet search such as www.content-analysis.de/ qualitative.html or www.researchware.com/resources/resources.html). On the other hand, if the amount of narrative is small and manageable, then that material could probably be typed into transcripts and analyzed manually.

Regardless of the volume of data or the type of approach that is used, the goal of qualitative data analysis is the same: to systematically examine text for primary themes to inform your needs assessment project. The process typically begins with entering all data (usually field notes, audio tapes, focus group notes, or notes from open-ended interviews) into a computerized system. The computer program may be one purchased specifically for qualitative data analysis, or it could be a regular word processing program such as Microsoft Word. The needs assessment team or investigator begins the process of reading text and identifying meaningful units of information.

Table 4.11 Example of a Matrix to Organize Qualitative Responses

Respondent	Response	Theme
Agency director	I feel that one of our most important resources is our domestic violence program. Our staff are well-trained and well-informed of the needs of clients in this community. No other agency provides these services.	**Domestic violence**
Treatment provider	I have been working here for about 6 months. My impression is that domestic violence is a big problem in this community. We see only the tip of the iceberg.	**Domestic violence**
Client	I came to this program with a serious problem. The counselors here have really helped me to see that I was using drugs to cope with the emotional and physical pain of domestic violence. That was my biggest problem.	**Domestic violence**

One way to organize the information might be through a matrix such as that shown in Figure 4.11, which features open-ended interview responses from multiple respondents in a residential substance abuse treatment program. The respondent and response fields are filled in from the transcript. The "theme" field is handwritten by the needs assessment team member as she goes through the transcript to code the data.

You can see from this matrix that there is a definite theme around the need and value of services in this agency to address domestic violence issues. The helpful thing about using this type of matrix to organize chunks of data is that the needs assessment team or investigator has the ability to code each block of data, and then go back and look for similarities and differences in the identified themes. These blocks of data can then be grouped into other, larger constructs or categories. This coding process is known as "open coding." This process can then be used to identify the themes and the transcript can be re-examined with those themes in mind.

The identified themes can be read or printed out so that the needs assessment team can check to make sure that they have grasped the meaning within each category as well as determined that the categories are not overlapping. The team may also decide to group the themes into "primary" and "secondary" categories, depending on the consistencies that are noted and the context for the responses. During this step, the investigator may read the passages composing each of the categories or themes multiple times, known as *constant comparative analysis*, as an iterative process to make sure that the identified theme is the best way to capture the meaning of the coded passages.

Qualitative data analysis can be frustrating for a needs assessment team because the themes that emerge are completely based on the reviewer's interpretation of findings, which may be biased by their own life experiences, knowledge, intuition about the data, and so forth. We recommend having several team members examine the data for key themes. This will help to eliminate the potential for biasing the data based on individual expectations. In addition, having multiple reviewers may also open additional perspectives on the needs assessment data that one reviewer may have missed.

Example of a Project Using Qualitative Analysis

Lewis et al. (2005) conducted a project in New Jersey to better understand the perceptions of intimate partner abuse in a Latino community. The team conducted focus groups with Latino community members and key informant interviews with community service providers. Transcripts were coded for primary themes, which were "deductive" (derived from the literature) and "inductive" (derived from reading the transcripts). Findings indicated that factors associated with intimate partner abuse included financial problems, substance abuse, immigration stress, relationship problems, family history of abuse, cultural norms of machismo and gender roles, and level of acculturation. Findings also indicated that intimate partner abuse was more accepted in Latino culture, which largely influenced victim reports and the opportunities for intervention. Other barriers for victim reporting included distrust of police officers, fear of harm from abuser, fear of losing children, lack of family support, and shame. Qualitative data were further analyzed to find a number of similarities in the perspectives of community members and service providers on the factors associated with abuse and barriers to reporting abusive episodes. The findings from this study indicate that there is value in collecting and analyzing data from multiple perspectives to gain a more comprehensive look at the community issues. The noted similarities and differences may have important implications for needs assessment researchers interested in this topic area.

The example above demonstrates how a qualitative analysis can be used in a needs assessment project.

Content Analysis

Another way of looking at data that lies somewhere between quantitative and qualitative approaches is content analysis. Specifically, content analysis involves searching for and counting key words, phrases, or concepts in communications. Key words or phrases may be counted (frequencies of occurrence), measured (e.g., the size of a newspaper article in column inches or the amount of time allocated to a specific topic in a speech), or otherwise categorized in a manner that others could replicate. Content analysis can be used either retrospectively (to examine materials already in existence) or prospectively (to analyze impending events or narratives).

Consider this scenario: A director of a substance abuse treatment program has recently begun to think about increasing the number of treatment beds in her agency that are designated for criminal justice referred clients. She has noticed a trend in monthly reports that the number of criminal justice referred clients has been gradually increasing. In addition, her staff has brought this issue to her attention, and it is a problem because current programming does not address the specific needs that these clients experience in treatment (i.e., problems getting a job due to felony convictions). The agency director decides to do a content analysis of transcripts from monthly staff meetings to attempt to identify other specific needs that these clients may be experiencing so that adjustments can be made in the current programming. Table 4.12 demonstrates steps that the agency director should take to conduct a content analysis.

Content analysis essentially consists of counting. The agency director and her student intern may find from the review of staff meeting minutes that in the last year there were 25 clients who were discussed as having no place to live, 43 who had employment problems, 14 with substance abuse issues, 3 with child custody issues, and 2 with medication adjustment problems. These results support the trend that was being observed in the monthly reports. Similarly, content analysis could also be used to count the number of editorials in the local newspaper addressing the problems of the homeless.

Content analysis can be used in conjunction with other qualitative analytic approaches to identify themes.

Application of Data Findings to Your Needs Assessment Project

This chapter has provided an overview of quantitative and qualitative approaches to data analysis for your needs assessment project. The analytic approach is largely contingent on the scope of the needs assessment project, the needs assessment design, the type of data that has been collected, and the question that needs to be addressed. Similar to selecting the right

Table 4.12 Steps to Guide a Content Analysis

Step 1	Framing a research question	What are the treatment needs of criminal justice referred clients?
Step 2	Deciding on source materials	Source material for this content analysis will include transcripts from agency staff meetings, which are audiotaped and transcribed into a Microsoft Word document.
Step 3	Deciding on units of analysis	The unit of analysis consists of the words indicating needs associated with "criminal justice" cases or clients. The agency director will count the number of times each need is mentioned and document the context for treatment needs that are described in the same phrases.
Step 4	Deciding on a sampling design	Because the agency director's time is limited, she will review the transcripts from staff meetings over the past 6 months.
Step 5	Counting the units of analysis	Counting identified treatment needs of the criminal justice referred clients mentioned in staff meetings.
Step 6	Conduct reliability checks	When she has completed her review of staff transcripts, she will ask a student intern to conduct the same analysis. If findings are similar, then the agency director can have increased confidence that her findings are reliable.

needs assessment design, there are also considerations with regard to data analysis and statistical expertise and resources within the needs assessment team that will affect the final product. For example, one survey could employ mostly closed-ended or multiple choice responses, but another survey might use only open-ended questions. The multiple choice response format will be easier to code and tabulate, lending itself to a quantitative type of analysis. Open-ended questions generally cannot be analyzed quantitatively. Along this line, the choice of variables and whether they are created at the nominal level ("My need for drug counseling services is 1. great or 2. small") or at the interval level ("Please rate your need for drug counseling services on a 1–100 scale") will also affect your analytic strategy.

The following table is provided as a resource for decisions about data analysis in relation to the needs assessment design. Although there may be special situations where these guidelines may not apply, for most cases

Example of a Qualitative Project Using Content Analysis

In a separate study, Daiski (2007) examined the health and health-care needs of homeless people in Canada. This study incorporated open-ended interviews and observational field notes with a sample of 24 homeless adults. Field note and interview transcripts were analyzed using a thematic content analysis. Analysis included counting the number of physical health problems and other treatment needs noted by homeless clients in their study. As expected, participants reported a number of health problems, such as seizure disorders, chronic respiratory problems, and muscle/bone problems (e.g., arthritis). Many participants reported difficulty sustaining employment, living in fear for their safety, and social isolation. In addition, a number of respondents reported substance abuse and mental health issues. Plans for using findings from this study included integrating outreach services for homeless individuals into community health centers, which may have important implications for needs assessment researchers. If you read this report you will note the absence of tables or statistical reporting—a hallmark of qualitative research.

Table 4.13   Guide for Selecting Data Analysis Approach

Data collection design	Type of data collected	Possible analysis
Focus Group	Open-ended questions, either field notes or audiotaped transcripts of responses	Qualitative; content analysis
Community Forum	Open-ended questions, either field notes or audio taped transcripts of responses	Qualitative; content analysis
Agency files – therapist narratives or progress notes	Field notes	Qualitative; content analysis
Agency files – therapist narratives or progress notes	MIS system data or needs assessment team event counts	Quantitative; univariate analysis
Surveys or interviews with nonstructured with open-ended responses	Open-ended questions, either field notes or audiotaped transcripts of responses	Qualitative; content analysis
Surveys or interviews with structured with close-ended responses	Either continuous or categorical data	Quantitative; univariate, bivariate, or multivariate analysis

the table will be helpful in guiding decisions about your analytic approach.

Although this table may serve as a guide to aligning the data analysis approach with the design, note that the analytic approach can also be influenced by the project's staffing resources, expertise, and time in the same way as the overall design is influenced by these factors.

Summary

This chapter provides guidance on managing the data for your needs assessment project. The chapter shows that there are numerous different approaches that can be used with both qualitative and quantitative data to identify patterns and main themes, to interpret, and to disseminate the findings of your project. Specifically, univariate (frequencies and measures of central tendency), bivariate (crosstabs, t-tests/ANOVAs, and correlations), and multivariate (regression) analyses can be used to examine numeric or numerically coded quantitative data. Content analysis and thematic coding were covered as approaches to examine qualitative data. After selecting the appropriate analytic technique and conducting the analysis, it is important to style the presentation of the data findings to the target audience for the needs assessment report, which will be discussed in the next chapter.

5

Writing the Needs
Assessment Report

This chapter will provide helpful suggestions for writing the needs assessment report and executive summary and will assist the reader in thinking about the stakeholders and other important persons who are in a position to use the findings to achieve the kind of changes needed for new services or to re-order budgetary priorities.

Audience and Writing Style

Before starting to write the first paragraph of the needs assessment report, it is important to remember the audience for whom the report is being written. Need assessment reports do not usually follow the academic style that you might use in writing for a college professor. Writing term papers or other academic writing usually involves the inclusion of multiple scholarly sources (e.g., a review of the literature) and may include a theoretical orientation or discussion of various theoretical perspectives. However, most need assessment reports are not written for professors, but for a nonacademic lay-reader. Because the needs assessment will be very specific to an agency, community, or problem in a given geographical region, it may not be necessary to review literature from scholarly sources; indeed, literature may not even exist or be specific enough to be relevant. Knowing the group for whom you are writing the report will help you adjust your writing style "up" to a more formal or scholarly style or "down" depending on the sophistication of those who will be reading your report.

Generally speaking, the writing should be aimed at the "average" reader—someone who has a high school degree. Most word processing programs have the ability to provide an estimate of the document's readability. If the readability index is at 12 or 13, then try to use shorter words and sentences to reduce it to 9, 10, or 11. Compound, complex sentences will increase the readability index. You should also avoid highly technical terms, jargon, and acronyms (e.g., SPSS) that might be unfamiliar to some of the audience.

Writing short sentences and composing short paragraphs (as opposed to those that stretch over a whole page) will assist in making the report more "reader-friendly" and easier to understand. Make the document easy to understand. Do not assume that the reader knows everything that you do. On the contrary, it is best to imagine that the reader has no knowledge of your project and to start from the very beginning and bring them along. Because you have been involved with the needs assessment project, you have an "insider's knowledge" that others will not have. If you are not careful, important details can be overlooked because you may forget that not everyone knows what you have learned. If you are on the needs assessment planning team, one way to avoid this problem is to keep a log or journal that records important decisions that were made and possibly the rationale for them. For example, the committee might decide to mail questionnaires not to former clients but only to current clients because of a limited budget. Because you were there and benefited from the discussion, it might not occur to you to explain in the report why clients with closed cases were excluded from the data collection.

At the same time, the needs assessment report should not contain superfluous information or present too many details that do not assist readers in understanding the project or its findings. It would not be necessary to note every decision, to list every fact, or to inundate the reader with all of the statistical tests of significance that were conducted.

Instead, keep in mind that most readers are not interested in long reports—especially those where the information they are most interested in reading about is difficult to find or buried deep in pointless trivia about the project's findings.

In academic writing, passive voice is often expected (e.g., "five focus groups were created"); however, writing in active voice (e.g., "the planning team interviewed eight agency supervisors") often makes for more interesting reading and helps to personalize the report. If you want your report to be read by many people in the agency or community, then it might be best to choose the active voice over the passive. This should be a topic discussed by the planning committee as should deciding who ought to receive copies of the report.

What Should the Needs Assessment Report Contain?

Need assessment reports contain four distinct components, which will each be discussed in turn.

The Introduction

All needs assessments should start by describing the problem that has given rise to the needs assessment project. Sometimes it is helpful to provide your readers with some statistics so that the problem can be considered in context. For example, in Crockett County the annual incidence of cervical cancer might be 16.2 cases per 100,000 population, whereas the national rate is 7.9 cases per 100,000—clearly, a problem worthy of attention.

Be sure to explain the purpose for the needs assessment. Sometimes this is expressed as a goal, objective, or rationale. If the needs assessment has come about because of some local tragedy (e.g., a teen suicide), then it would be okay to inform readers about that case or story. Remember that those reading your report may not be familiar with the impetus or motivation for the needs assessment as you. When they have finished reading this section, they should have a good idea about the problem or issue, the rationale for studying it, and what you hope to learn from the needs assessment.

The Methodology

As we learned earlier, the methodology of a needs assessment refers to the what, how, and when of the data collection process. In other words, you will need to explain what procedures you used, how your participants were recruited into the project, what questions were asked of them and so forth. Normally, you would identify the instruments that you used to collect data and you might want to provide a brief description of them or cite a reference where readers could find additional information if desired. Here you would also discuss how many questionnaires were distributed, the number of surveys returned, and that sort of thing. Enough information should be provided that the reader can understand the data collection strategy and its rigor.

The reader of this section of your report will be interested in whom you contacted and how you collected your data. Did you mail out questionnaires to staff? To clients? Distribute them to passers-by at the mall? Conduct focus groups with prospective clients? Interview key informants in the community? You owe it to your readers to explain how many persons were contacted or involved, the response or return rates on your surveys, and/or estimates of those who chose not to participate. If your data collection design was scientifically constructed (e.g., you did a random selection, probability sample with a margin of error and level of confidence), then briefly explain your random selection procedure. Append a copy of your questionnaire or interview schedule at the end of the needs assessment report. If you have borrowed a questionnaire or data collection instrument used in some other study, then inform the reader about that. If your needs assessment planning team created the data collection instrument, then you might want to inform the reader about that process—who had input and who reviewed or critiqued the instrument.

Even if your design is more inferential and less scientific, readers of your report will want to know how you chose to interview or question the respondents whom you asked to participate. The sample is a representation of those in the larger population (all of those who potentially might have been contacted), and readers will expect to know how these "representatives" were chosen to speak about their or the program's needs.

Also of interest will be who collected the data (e.g, external contractor or agency staff) and their relationship to the agency as well as how much involvement the needs assessment investigator or team had with those supplying the information. For example, was the interview a 15-minute interview? Did the focus groups last 2 hours on average? Were the surveys anonymous? Did the majority of the staff participate?

If your needs assessment will involve a sophisticated data analysis or at least more than reporting percentages, then you may want to briefly describe your data analytic plan either at the end of the methodology section or the beginning of the findings section.

The Findings

The main reason for reading the needs assessment report is to learn what the needs assessment team discovered. You may want to give this section considerable thought in terms of how you organize your findings. For example, you might want to discuss what you think is the most important finding first, and then the second most, and so on. Or, you might organize the findings by some kind of topical arrangement—those relevant to children under the age of 18 years, adults, older adults, and so forth.

In a large community, the findings could be organized by neighborhood or topical problem (e.g., crime, garbage collection, schools, etc.). The presentation of the findings is directly related to the purpose of the needs assessment and what you hope to accomplish with your report. Before you actually start the writing of this section you may wish to take a blank sheet of paper, write the purpose of the needs assessment on the top of it, and then begin to list your findings that most directly relate.

The results or findings section of your report should summarize what you have learned from the data. In some ways, your task with this section is not unlike that of the prospector looking for gold. You don't need to inform the reader about every rock or pebble that you come across. In other words, it is *not* necessary to inform the reader of every small fact that you might have uncovered (e.g., there are three more 90-year-olds living in zip code 40019 than in zip code 40017). If you have a lot of numerical data, then presenting the data in easy-to-comprehend tables is usually a good strategy. The rule here is that "less is more." In other words, instead of preparing 35 full-page tables of tabular data, you will have more people read your report if you prepare, say, no more than five or six tables. Similarly, you will have more readers of your tables if you don't cram too much information into each one, making them overly complex and difficult to comprehend. Although the natural tendency is to want to inform the reader about *everything*, remember that each reader's time is valuable and that most don't want to spend all afternoon delving into some fine point of data analysis. *Show* your readers what is important by what you present in your tables. *Tell* your reader about your key findings in your written narrative.

If the story does not seem to flow easily, then it may be that you are looking at the numbers (e.g., 233 men and 187 women) instead of the *percentages* or the *proportions* of clients or respondents who are stating a preference or identifying a problem. Often the numbers of men and women may not be comparable. It is not possible to obtain men and women in exactly the same number. Proportion is important. For example, if 75% of the male respondents and 90% of females say that there are too many gun-related crimes in the community, that is a pretty powerful statement that should be discussed. Proportions communicate beautifully and sometimes more powerfully than more sophisticated analyses.

Another approach you might be able to use in telling the story is to see if there are comparable statistics (benchmarks) from national, state, or other local organizations. It could be that compared to the national average, the problem in your community is three times greater. Or perhaps people in the adjoining county recognize the problem in approximately the same proportion. Similar findings as produced by the benchmarks serve to give readers (and you!) some assurance that your findings are not a wild or random fluke.

When you finish your first draft of the findings section, go back over it to see if there is too much repetition. For example, you may not always need to use tables to present data that can be easily explained in the narrative section. To take an example, citizens of Twowheel City may feel that lack of bicycle lanes is the number one problem in their community. It may not be necessary to create tables to show the number of people who endorsed that notion by gender, census tract, age group, and ethnic group. On the other hand, your analysis of the data might show that young adults (ages 19–39 years) spoke to that problem exclusively, whereas other age groups identified different problems and with far less agreement. You may have found that persons ages 40 to 60 years felt that the greatest community need was for a recreational center for teenagers, and that adults age 61 years and older wanted more retail shopping options downtown. Sometimes it is important to use a table to show that certain needs cluster more in one group than in another.

If you involve hypothesis testing (e.g., t-tests, chi-squares, etc.), keep in mind that showing the average reader of your report the statistical results (e.g., X^2 [6, n = 997] = 4.39; p = 0.61) will perplex and confuse many. It is better to state that "a significant difference" was found or that "no significant differences" were found with regard to your analysis and let it go at that. If you feel that it is necessary to report out the statistical information, another option would be to insert this information in an appendix at the end of the report.

Reporting Findings versus Making Recommendations

Early in the planning process, a decision will have to be made in the writing of the needs assessment report regarding whether the report will present the findings objectively and factually and allow the reader to draw his or her own conclusions or whether the document will state a set of conclusions or recommendations that should be implemented. If your needs assessment planning committee is also part of an advocacy group, then the decision to conclude the report with a series of recommendations may be a natural and logical way to end.

One cautionary note is that you should be careful to not let your exuberance or strong sense of advocacy interfere with your objective judgment when writing conclusions or recommendations. Don't hang a major recommendation on a weak piece of data (e.g., one client said, "The receptionist never answers the telephone."). In scholarly writing, sometimes this problem is discussed as "overgeneralizing." If you are going to draw a conclusion or make an important recommendation, then base it on sound data reasonably gathered with integrity. Do not "cherry-pick" the data items that support your position and ignore or overlook the items that do not. If three of five items do not support your advocacy stance and only two do, it would be unfair and unprofessional to focus only on the two. It would be better to share with the reader that the results were "mixed" or not definitive.

Some social scientists feel that the data "should speak for itself" and that the investigator's role is simply to gather the best data that can be acquired in that situation and not to make policy or program decisions. This stance is because researchers know that one's own values and beliefs can influence how data are interpreted and even how questions are framed. For some researchers, the citizens living in a community or service providers, or both, are in a better position to know what needs to change in terms of local programming and policies.

It would make perfect sense to clarify with your boss, the sponsor of the needs assessment, or others critically involved in the planning of the needs assessment before you begin collecting data as to the expectations regarding the final report. You might even wish to create a memo, letter, or some other document that precisely states the goals, objectives, or purpose of the needs assessment, the time frame, the resources available, the length of the final report (ballpark estimate), and whether or not conclusions/recommendations should be drafted. You might even want to draft an outline of the proposed sections in the report to avoid possible misunderstanding later. (If you are conducting the needs assessment as a hired consultant, then the memo would also be a good place to document the fee that you will be paid.)

Finally, if you (or the needs assessment planning team) are uncomfortable making recommendations or drawing major conclusions from the data, then another alternative would be to frame decisions and choices that are available to the agency directors, governing board, and so forth. Agencies may become defensive if the needs assessment findings are negative—for example, if staff are not adhering to stated agency policy or if their efforts are viewed by clients as ineffectual. Sometimes these issues can be defused by preparing a draft of the findings and giving persons in power (e.g., the agency director) a preview of these prior to "finalizing" the report. Trusted staff and others in the agency can also provide useful feedback and may be able to suggest a way to present results more diplomatically than originally drafted.

Limitations of the Report

Every research effort is somewhat imperfect and therefore bounded by its limitations. In other words, no study is completely free of bias, and most have experienced some problems—either major or minor—in the data collection. When the needs assessment has been poorly conceptualized (e.g, a single focus group of six teenagers is used to represent all of Chicago), the writer or writers of the needs assessment report should be aware that the needs assessment has a major limitation and consequently be very conservative and cautious when discussing the findings. On the other hand, when the needs assessment effort has been well-planned and -executed, then one can have much more confidence about the findings and should be less concerned with minor limitations. The study would also have a major limitation if a survey questionnaire was mailed to many potential respondents but experienced a minuscule response rate (e.g., mailed to 1,000 potential respondents but only 57 responded). There are many ways that a study can be flawed; any violation of good research procedures would constitute a limitation (e.g., discovering after the data had been obtained that the questionnaire was biased—see the example).

What is a minor limitation? It is a flaw or error, not easily corrected or detected later, that probably would not change the results. For example, after constructing a sample frame of clients who visited the agency in 2008, randomly selecting their names, and mailing out to 650 different persons, the investigator learned that clients who entered the agency between May 1 and May 15 had not been added to the database because of the program assistant being on vacation and no one entering the data during her absence. There is no reason to suspect that the loss of clients from the survey during that 2-week period would significantly alter the findings of the needs assessment. By contrast, there could be seasonal variations in client flow. Program staff serving children with mental health issues might find that clients admitted during the summer months presented with

---

> ### Example of a Limitation Stemming from a Flawed Questionnaire Item
> Please rate the quality of the services provided by the agency:
> ☐ Excellent
> ☐ Very Good
> ☐ Good
> ☐ Poor
> Comment: This questionnaire item is flawed because it isn't balanced. Clients have three opportunities to say something good about the program and only one opportunity to indicate that services were not of good quality. Thus, it is much more likely that respondents will give good ratings to this item even if the services were not all that great. One should not conclude from this one item that the agency is doing a fine job and doesn't need to work on the quality of its services. If this item were heavily relied on in the study (there were no other similar items to back it up), then the study would have a limitation. It is less of a problem if there are other items getting at the same content.

more severe problems than clients admitted during the school year. In that situation, the loss of 2 or 3 weeks of client data (using the example of a secretary on vacation) could become a major limitation if the random sample is much less likely to represent clients with severe problems.

The Executive Summary

An executive summary is an abbreviated needs assessment report. It provides an overview containing the essence of the report without all of the details. The notion here is that busy individuals can be provided with a quick synopsis or highlights of the report without having to read the whole document.

There are just a few tips for writing an executive summary. First, do not attempt to write it before the full needs assessment report is finished. The executive summary must reflect what the larger report contains and should not present any new information.

Second, although the executive summary is similar to an abstract, it is much longer than the half a page or six to eight sentences that might characterize a typical abstract. As a rule of thumb, you should aim for your executive summary to be about 3 to 4 pages long and certainly no longer than 9 to 10 pages. Generally speaking, there is no reason to insert or reproduce tables or graphics contained in the larger report. It is often helpful, however, to use bullet points to make the report easier to digest at a glance.

A third tip is to model the summary after the major sections contained in full report. If your larger report contains an introduction, methodology, findings, and recommendations section, then the executive summary should as well and in the same order. If the reader of the executive summary has a question about something in one of the sections, then it should be easy for him or her to find the corresponding narrative in the full report.

Fourth, once again it is important to understand the audience for whom you are writing. Will it be a lay-audience (e.g., the "average" citizen, clients of the agency)? Expert service providers? Government officials? Consider how each of these groups might have different perspectives and background knowledge about the needs assessment. No matter who your audience is, be respectful in your writing style and always proofread to eliminate grammatical and organizational problems.

Disseminating the Findings of the Needs Assessment

There is essentially one major decision to be made concerning disseminating the needs assessment report and then minor decisions that follow. The major decision is whether the report is intended for "internal" use (e.g., to be read only by those within the organization or agency) or whether the findings will be shared with a wide readership of persons outside the organization or agency (e.g., possible funding sources, government officials, the local newspaper).

Reports intended only for internal use probably tend to be more informal because there is a more limited readership and many of these may know something about the problem or the reason for the needs assessment. Internal dissemination can be made by memo or E-mail attachment, and reports can be distributed at staff meetings where they can be explained. With internal dissemination there is probably a greater chance that someone with a question could get it answered informally by talking within the agency, possibly with someone on the planning team—perhaps even over a cup of coffee or at lunch.

Although it is a large generalization, needs assessment reports that are distributed externally probably tend to be glossier and more formal with more attention paid to their appearance and to the details of the needs assessment. They can be distributed at a news conference or made available to the public requesting a copy. However, it is much more likely that executive summaries will be read by the general public or the media, and typically many more of these are prepared for distribution than the full reports.

If you are in an advocacy role and believe that it is important for as many people as possible to be informed about your needs assessment, then besides holding a news conference you may want to mail copies of the executive summary to all of the radio and television stations and to all of the community groups or organizations that could possibly have an interest. Another possibility would be to post the report and executive summary on the agency's Web site so that it can be easily found.

Examples of executive summaries and reports can be found at:

☐ Rock County Wisconsin Community Needs Assessment
http://www.unitedwayjanesville.org/files/Executive%20Summary %20-%20Needs%20Assessment.pdf

☐ Greater Topeka
http://www.unitedwaytopeka.org/cnas.html

☐ Howard County, Indiana
http://www.unitedwayhoco.org/needs/ExecSummary07.pdf

☐ Rappahannock, Virginia
http://www.rappahannockunitedway.org/community/needs_ assessment.html

☐ Montgomery County, Pennsylvania
http://www.mcfoundationinc.org/pdfs/Montco_Needs_ExSum.pdf

☐ United Way of the Capital Region (with Latino Community Assessment)
http://www.uwcr.org/site/solutions/assessment.asp

☐ Chenango United Way
http://www.chenangouw.org/impact.html

☐ United Way of Metropolitan Nashville
http://www.tnstate.edu/ober/doc/Executive%20Summary-%20UW. doc

Summary

This chapter has provided guidance on how to prepare a needs assessment report that could be disseminated locally to a broad audience or internally within an agency. In the next two chapters we will turn our attention to specialized types of needs assessment. Chapter 6 will present a discussion of staff needs assessment conducted within an agency, whereas Chapter 7 will examine the processes involved in conducting a large scale, statewide effort.

6

Staff Training Needs Assessment

This chapter discusses the application of the needs assessment process within an organizational context. Social workers frequently assume administrative responsibilities soon after obtaining their MSWs. As social work managers, it is necessary at times to determine what skills or knowledge staff have or need. A staff training needs assessment is a specialized application of needs assessment that requires good familiarity and experience with the organization, its personnel, and programs. This chapter will present a needs assessment planning framework for identifying and discussing the key elements of the staff training needs assessment. It will also examine factors to consider when designing the process, strategies for assessing staff training needs, as well as precipitants for conducting a staff needs assessment.

Organizational problems such as unfilled staff vacancies and heavy client caseloads can often prevent long term planning, particularly when resources are thin, demands high, and time is short—conditions frequently found in social service organizations. In light of these constraints, the idea of conducting a staff training needs assessment could be met with a skeptical, "Why bother?" Managers and administrators often assume that they know what their staff needs and that they can implement staff training more efficiently by side-stepping a needs assessment, a process they may view as cumbersome, unwieldy, and perhaps too costly. However, although taking the time to survey staff requires additional effort, in the long run a needs assessment can be of great value to an organization. For example, it can support professional development and cultivate staff buy-in and readiness for coming organizational changes. How staff handle change is influenced by their perceptions of factors such as the agency's resources, work atmosphere, client needs, and work-related pressures (Simpson, 2002). Organizations that are not functioning well can experience greater difficulty when implementing change (Simpson, 2002). Involving staff at the beginning of the change process can help cultivate the cooperative work environment necessary for successful alterations in programs or policies.

Utilization of a systematic planning approach can provide reliable data to shape educational and training efforts that assist with the provision of high-quality services. Research suggests that the degree to which staff transfer new learning from educational training to practice can be greatly influenced by the agency's effort to proactively assess organizational and staff needs (Milne & Roberts, 2002). Adequate preplanning and assessment can provide the data needed to guide choices about educational content, instruction methods, and formats and can help gage staff receptivity—elements that can assist organizations in offering training that can be translated into practice.

Because a needs assessment is a *process* as well as a *product,* there are many elements that need to be considered when developing and implementing this strategy. A process that is well-developed and compatible with the agency climate and staff characteristics can yield a strong and useful assessment product.

Mapping Out a Needs Assessment Framework

As with any organizational strategy or change effort, it is helpful to have a framework or a "blueprint" to guide the development of a staff training needs assessment. Chapter 2 provided a foundation for thinking about elements important to address and consider when designing a needs assessment. This section extends that discussion and draws upon other research in examining recommended steps for designing a needs assessment focused on staff development and training. These steps are presented in Figure 6.1.

Although this model shows various needs assessment steps as being discrete, it is essential to remember that in reality the separation between activities is not always so clear. This chapter will discuss these steps in progression, but in practice, some of these stages may overlap or occur simultaneously. In addition, evaluation of the impact of training efforts may identify other deficits or problems that may require another needs

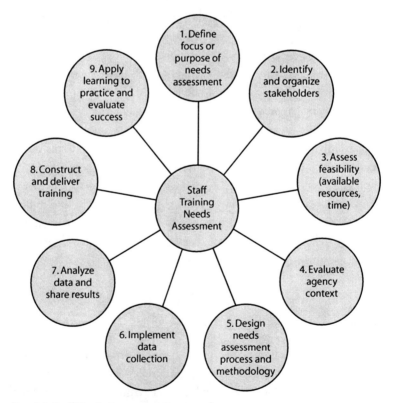

Figure 6.1 Staff Needs Assessment Framework

Example 1: Supporting a Mission Change

A private practice traditionally offered long-term individual and group therapy. With the advent of managed care, it became important for the practitioners to have the flexibility to employ brief therapy models because many clients had reimbursement for only a few sessions; their needs could not be adequately met with the existing services. Following an informal needs assessment involving an in-depth discussion with each of the practitioners, it became clear that past training and education did not prepare the therapists to effectively engage clients with brief therapy. An intensive training plan was developed and classes arranged in which all therapists participated. Once this training was complete, the agency mission shifted to include brief therapy as a treatment modality.

---

assessment process. Approaching the planning stage of needs assessment with flexibility and ongoing evaluation of its progress will assist you in responding to the unique needs and circumstances of the staff and organization. With this understanding, let's begin to review the steps outlined in the framework.

Step One: Defining the Purpose or Focus of a Needs Assessment

The purpose of a needs assessment is connected to the circumstances motivating it. There are a variety of challenges organizations encounter that can serve as a catalyst for a staff training needs assessment. These conditions can include the following.

A Shift in the Organizational Mission

The needs of a community or a consumer group can change, and consequently, the current service structure may no longer be adequate. In such a situation, it is possible staff may not be prepared for the new service direction without additional training. Because staff members with varied levels of skills and experience are what one commonly encounters, it is in the organization's best interest to conduct a needs assessment of staff members to be impacted by a forthcoming departmental or program change to determine if knowledge and skill gaps exist so that training efforts can be designed to address them.

A Shift in Funding Requirements

Some agencies and programs are funded by "soft money" —funds that are obtained from grants, foundations, or other such sources. These monies come with a mandate or expectation that they be used for a certain purpose or to meet the needs of a specific group. Agencies are then required to work within the parameters of these guidelines, and staff are hired with these services and goals in mind. However, funding sources, too, can experience a shift in mission or focus that can then impact the receiving agency. The shift may be one that existing staff can easily absorb, or it may be one that requires additional preparation. A needs assessment is helpful in determining what will be needed to continue to deliver services under new circumstances.

Another instance when this might occur is if a usual funding source is no longer available and the organization must seek funding elsewhere to continue to operate. New funding possibilities may be discovered that require shifts in services provided or populations served or may require the addition of a new service to meet all the requirements of the funding source. For example, a community mental health center receiving a substantially lower amount of county funds than anticipated one fiscal year searched for new funding sources. One service they already staffed was a crisis hotline. Building on this service, they were able to secure funding for the agency by adding a national helpline that expanded the issues they covered. The new helpline necessitated a needs assessment (conducted with focus groups and discussion), which in turn led to modifications in staff training.

Accreditation Requirements

Often service providers are accredited by outside regulatory organizations that are responsible for setting practice standards for specific areas of care and monitoring compliance with the standard (e.g., medical settings are accredited by the Joint Commission on Accreditation of Healthcare Organizations; JCAHO). Changes in organizational regulations may necessitate modification or change in procedure and service delivery in the workplace. Because the purpose of accreditation concerns quality of care and reassurance to the public that services have been evaluated and assessed as adequate, it is important to carefully assess staff training. If changes resulting from new regulations are extensive, central to client safety, or essential to service quality or delivery, then it may be necessary to conduct a needs assessment as a first step in preparing and educating staff to successfully meet the challenge of these changes.

Culture Shift or Policy Change

Organizations may experience critical incidents (e.g., a client's suicide, death of a child in foster care) or the documentation of inadequate care that immediately results in a new policy or procedure being implemented. It may be tempting for managers to make assumptions about what additional education is needed to address skill deficits, cultivate different intervention responses, or smoothly implement new policy. However, a needs assessment of staff is important under these circumstances for a couple of reasons. First, it provides the training program with a firm foundation of accurate data. Second, including the staff at the beginning of the change process with a needs assessment can help to increase their investment and reduce resistance when new expectations are implemented.

Example 2: Supporting a Change in Practice

At a medical trauma center, a manager observed that many staff in one department routinely treated patients who experienced sexual assault by briefing them on routine procedural aspects of care rather than providing supportive counseling. Further observation revealed two staff members who provided the expected supportive counseling interventions. These staff members were enlisted to help address and rectify the problem. They assessed other team members to better understand why supportive counseling wasn't being provided and asked their colleagues' about their comfort with the specific skills required to offer supportive counseling interventions. This appraisal identified skill deficits and time pressures as the root causes of this problem. The two staff members designed a training session that targeted skills that their team identified as weak and created a script and intervention outline other staff could follow when working with patients during high-volume, high-pressure work days. To support this shift in culture, they also served as ongoing resources for the staff.

Strategic Planning and Service Expansion

The delivery of social services is impacted by many factors, including local crises, changing demographics within a community, economic conditions, as well as changing client needs. Strategic planning is a frequently employed management strategy that assists with envisioning the future of an organization as well as perpetuating its growth and development (Chrislip, 2002). At times, a strategic plan requires a new investment in the human capital of the organization to achieve goals—a circumstance under which a needs assessment would be helpful.

A staff training needs assessment can also be helpful in instances where a new treatment model will be implemented or pilot tested in response to the identification of new community needs. Accurate identification of staff training needs prior to offering the new treatment model affords staff the opportunity to receive adequate preparation. Taking this extra step would be especially important if the treatment model itself will be evaluated for effectiveness; targeted staff training can help ensure treatment fidelity (integrity) and help control for the impact that poorly prepared staff could otherwise have on treatment outcomes.

Organizational Downsizing and Restructuring

Funding cuts and mission shifts may necessitate the downsizing of staff or services or the restructuring of staff responsibilities and job duties. These circumstances may place staff remaining with the organization in the position of assuming new job responsibilities that may be quite different from those they were initially hired to fill. In addition, organizations facing funding cuts are better situated with employees who are versatile and cross-trained in jobs other than that for which they are primarily responsible. Changes in job positions or responsibilities suggest the need to comprehensively assess staff readiness and their ability to make the required shift.

Staff Enrichment

Organizations can settle into a routine, and staff can become complacent with the status quo. Although this situation may reduce stress, employees may miss opportunities for growth and development and become unprepared to face new challenges. Professional development can be viewed as enrichment of staff and can assist with improving staff morale. A staff needs assessment can allow staff to specify what content and skill areas they wish to develop. Such an assessment can also be used to identify barriers to education and preferred training strategies (See the Appendix for an example of such a needs assessment.)

Step Two: Identify and Organize Stakeholders

Milne and Roberts (2002) diagramed steps important to the planning of staff education and noted that the first is to procure support in the workplace by gathering key personnel and important stakeholders. Determining who would be appropriate to include on the needs assessment team will be somewhat dependent on the nature of the problem, as well as the dynamics and structure of the organization. Possible *stakeholders* would include anyone who contributes to the problem, is impacted by the issue, has expertise or information that can help generate a solution or plan, or with power to either support or obstruct the project (Chrislip, 2002). To design a needs assessment method that stands the best chance of providing good information, stakeholders should be diverse in perspective and involvement with the problem. Because staff cooperation and buy-in are essential for successful application of training content to practice, including staff at the start of the planning process is recommended. In addition, thought should be given to the selection of individual participants. Personal characteristics or work habits and committee size (*see* Chapter 2) can influence the productivity of the group.

Step Three: Assess Feasibility

As discussed in Chapter 2, factors such as the amount budgeted for the needs assessment, the availability of staff resources, the urgency of the problem to be addressed, and the time constraints all need to be considered relative to the feasibility of the project. This step can serve as a "reality check" at an early point in the planning process. Establishing what resources are possible to use and defining the limits and scope of the needs assessment will provide the necessary structure for those beginning to make plans for the assessment.

Step Four: Evaluate Agency Context

Prior to formulating and carrying out a staff development needs assessment, it is helpful to conduct a broader assessment that explores characteristics of the environmental context. Milne and Roberts (2002) refer to this as an "organizational needs assessment" (p. 155). Information gathered in this step can help planners remember the larger picture (i.e., resources, obstacles, staff and organizational limitations or strengths) that can be used to inform the construction of the subsequent staff needs assessment (Rowan-Sal, Greener, Joe, & Simpson, 2007) and assist in the successful implementation of training efforts that follow (Courtney, Joe, Rowan-Szal, & Simpson, 2007). As discussed in Chapter 3, there is an array of approaches that can be utilized for the needs assessment. The one chosen in any one situation should be compatible with the organization and departmental dynamics. Contextual and organizational elements that need to be considered and evaluated when making needs assessment decisions will be explored below. When reviewing these factors, keep in mind that it is possible that important attributes of the organization may not be well-known or understood prior to a needs assessment. If this is the case, then the needs assessment itself can be constructed to include items that assist in gathering important information about the characteristics of the environment that may impact training (Rowan-Szal et al. 2007). There are six aspects of the agency context that may influence the staff needs assessment.

The Organization's Vision, Mission, and Goals

Departmental and individual staff goals should flow from and be compatible with the organization's overall vision, mission, and strategic plan. The actual *content* of the needs assessment should consider these organizational elements so that staff responses are relevant to the needs and future of the agency. For example, if the mission of the agency is to provide safety net services for the homeless and to make referrals to other agencies for specialized needs, then it would be inappropriate to ask staff if they are interested in learning about eye movement desensitization and reprocessing therapy; questions such as this may confuse staff regarding the agency's mission and divert the department from the focus of the agency rather than moving it forward. Revisiting the organization's mission also creates the opportunity to check for possible *mission drift* that could have occurred over the years (Brody, 2006). Clarifying the actual mission and the anticipated future direction of the organization before constructing the needs assessment will support the gathering of useful and relevant information.

The Organization's Culture and Values

Organizations develop a culture of their own that embodies the traditions, attitudes, core values, and practices central to the agency. The culture that is present in an organization influences staff behavior as well as their ideas and beliefs about how things should be done. It is necessary to consider the established culture and guiding values when planning the questions for the needs assessment as well as when deciding on a process. The process should fit staff expectations about how things are done to support trust in the endeavor and the data. Working within the culture will serve to increase staff trust and buy-in of the activity, decrease resistance, and, in turn, increase the reliability and accuracy of the data collected.

Management Leadership Style

In addition to organizational culture and values so, too, can the leadership style of the manager influence staff's performance and job-related behaviors and beliefs. The manager has a primary role in shaping staff's perception of what is valued and acceptable in an organization, and leadership style can greatly impact the infrastructure in a department (Brody, 2006). Although circumstances will call for different leadership styles according to situational factors, managers and supervisors may tend to employ one leadership style over another, which can affect communication and interaction patterns. Leadership style can also contribute to what staff members have come to expect in the work setting. Accounting for this variable and keeping usual leadership style in mind while designing a needs assessment process can help the activity feel like a natural extension of regular daily activities, which can fuel trust in the effort and help ensure better accuracy of the data.

Leadership styles have been described in a variety of terms in the literature. One such description by Brody (2006) constructs three leadership style categories: directive, participative, and delegative. These categories divide power and authority between the leader and the staff differently, a dynamic that is important to consider when choosing a needs assessment strategy. An authoritative leader will retain decision-making power, whereas the participatory leader will seek input from staff before making decisions. The delegative leader abdicates decision-making authority and allows staff the power to both inform and make decisions. The decision-making approach that is most predominant in the agency's administrative structure should be accounted for when formulating plans for implementing a needs assessment and carrying it out. Remember, for the data to be reliable, staff members need to trust the process. If the usual standard in the workplace is that staff members are involved in making departmental decisions, then a needs assessment that is developed without their input runs the risk of resistance and lack of commitment to the process.

Compatibility with the Work Environment Characteristics

Methods for conducting needs assessments include observation of staff, focus groups, individual interviews, staff surveys, and consultations with outside experts. These approaches vary in terms of the funding they require, the extent of intrusion they involve, and the amount of staff time and participation they necessitate. When deciding on an assessment method, all of these elements need to be considered within the work context.

For example, if a manager wishes to conduct a needs assessment with a staff of 120 service providers who work one of three shifts and provide daily coverage at a very busy hospital, the best method of assessment may be one that utilizes a written survey. This method requires a small time investment of each staff member (out of respect for their already demanding workload) and allows each employee the opportunity to participate (as it will be available to staff despite the shift or day of the week they are scheduled to work). In another case, a treatment team in a small community mental health center that consists of one manager and seven therapists who have a work routine that includes weekly staff meetings might feel that a group discussion to determine training needs is more natural.

Dynamics of the Staff

Because the purpose of the staff needs assessment is to obtain reliable data that can be used to address staff development and training needs, it is important to consider any staff dynamics that can compromise or influence the accuracy of the data staff supply. For example, let's return to the example of the team of seven therapists who work in a community mental health center. At first blush, the best choice for a needs assessment method appears to be the use of a group discussion. However, when assessing team dynamics (the way the team works together and relates to one another), let's say that an outside person observes that two therapists dominate the staff meetings and intimidate the others. As a result, only these two staff members air their ideas and opinions because others do not experience the acceptance, safety, and trust necessary to risk sharing their thoughts or asking questions. Under these circumstances, it is contraindicated to use a focus group approach because the data collection method will not yield good data from all participants. Despite the small staff size, a confidential survey that includes questions that ask about training needs in the areas of communication and teamwork might be a better choice. Team dynamics greatly influence the openness of the work environment and the quality and quantity of information shared within the group and must be considered when planning for a staff needs assessment.

Intentions of and Motivations for the Needs Assessment

Although the end-point of a staff training needs assessment is to determine the areas in which to focus training efforts, motivations for conducting needs assessments can differ. As discussed previously, needs assessments can be utilized to *(a)* determine the extent of a problem noticed during a few observations; *(b)* identify areas for professional development to increase staff morale; *(c)* inventory strengths and deficits in staff abilities and knowledge when facing impending organizational changes; and *(d)* challenge the "status quo" and increase the depth or quality of services provided. The impetus for conducting the needs assessment also needs to be considered when designing the process.

As an illustration, if a supervisor wishes to empower and enrich his or her staff by expanding professional development opportunities, then it might be best to include staff representatives beginning with the first step of planning so that their inclusion in all facets of the decision-making and planning processes communicates the intention to enrich and empower them. The way one goes about making decisions and involving others (or not) communicates values and leadership style and constitutes some of the information staff evaluate when forming their perceptions of culture and their value to the organization. Describing a process that demonstrates to staff through action their role and importance in this project can also serve to enhance their investment and commitment to the project.

Step Five: Design the Needs Assessment Process and Methodology

As we have stressed before, staff buy-in and investment are necessary for both obtaining accurate data and successfully identifying gaps in knowledge and skill. It is important to remember that the end-point of a needs assessment is not gathering the data but being able to use the data to address a deficit and improve staff performance and quality of service. To achieve this aim, the cooperation of those participating in training and delivering services is essential. Although involving staff as much as possible in all steps of this planning process has been recommended, the degree to which this is possible may vary; the best strategy may not always emphasize staff input and involvement throughout the entire process. Certain situations and circumstances discussed below suggest the use of different approaches depending on the nature and scope of the problem to be addressed, the urgency of the situation, and the characteristics and dynamics of the context within which the needs assessment will occur. Each time a needs assessment is designed, it is important to evaluate it in response to a unique problem, so that the best strategy is chosen and staff is afforded the maximum level of input circumstances can allow.

In the following section, various planning and implementation strategies are reviewed, beginning with the approach that utilizes the least amount of staff input.

The "Top-down" Management Approach

In a "top-down" approach, the manager designs a needs assessment with no or minimal input from others. A decision to implement a "top-down" process can be a response to reviewing existing agency data, the presence of a clear-cut, well-focused need (e.g., implementation of a very specific policy change), or an urgent crisis situation for which timeliness is an issue (e.g., an imminent nursing strike during which social workers may need to be outsourced to other hospitals within the health-care system to avoid layoff). A needs assessment utilizing the "top-down" approach is one that can be formulated and implemented quickly because there is no need for consensus building or discussion. Thoughtful consideration should be given to the decision to use this approach so that it is used effectively and not to the detriment of the departmental culture. Successful implementation of this approach requires that the manager be confident in his or her understanding of the problem and the knowledge and skill areas necessary to include in the needs assessment.

Establishing a consistent pattern of "top-down" needs assessment places the manager in the role of "expert" and can be experienced as devaluing staff input. This can have a negative impact on staff morale that may make sought-after improvements more difficult to obtain. Managers who react from individual perceptions of a problem without input from others can increase the risk of misperceptions of the problem. Collaborative decision-making can empower staff and increase their investment and ownership of the problem as well as the solution.

Management Team Planning

In settings where there are multiple managers who are responsible for different areas of service, there is an opportunity to construct a needs assessment that incorporates various viewpoints—especially if these managers come from different disciplines (i.e., social work, psychology, rehabilitation counseling, occupational therapy). Inclusion of diverse perspectives can allow for a thorough examination of the problem and further broadens the perspective. This approach depends on more input from others than the previous one but again only utilizes the management viewpoint and is an "outside-looking-in" perspective. This may be a viable option for organizations in which trust is high and relations good between management and staff because staff will need to feel comfortable with management representing their viewpoints. If this type of relationship is not in place across all units or teams and a collaborative approach is desired, then it may be best to pursue a strategy that directly involves staff members in the planning process, such as the collaborative committee planning or team process models discussed below.

Collaborative Committee Planning

In this approach, a collaborative committee is formed to design and oversee the needs assessment process. Depending on the composition of staff asked to participate in the needs assessment, this committee may consist of participants of the same discipline or contain representatives from various disciplines affected by the change or issue. The primary difference between this approach and the management team approach is that this strategy allows for participation of group members regardless of their standing in the organizational hierarchy. Directors, managers, and direct service staff are all represented in the membership of the committee, thus giving voice to each perspective as the needs assessment is created. A question to ask that may be useful in determining whether this approach would be appropriate is, "What personnel are essential for successful implementation of the upcoming change?" If the answer consists of staff from various disciplines and different levels of responsibility within the organization, then the optimal committee membership should reflect this diversity. Although this approach allows staff to be involved in the planning of a needs assessment, the team process model may be a better choice if there is an opportunity to increase staff involvement and the problem impacts predominantly one department or team.

The Team Process Model

The team process model, a strategy that is compatible with both the participatory and delegative leadership styles, involves staff members at the very first step of planning the needs assessment. Once a problem area is identified or suspected, staff members are immediately asked to become involved in the planning process. Along with management, staff members work together to refine the definition of the problem, assess feasibility of the needs assessment, discuss other members necessary to the assessment team, contribute their understanding of the organizational context, and assist with designing, implementing, and disseminating assessment results. The actual input and role of management may vary depending on the function and investment of staff in the needs assessment and training project. For example, on some teams, management and staff members may assume equal responsibility for planning and carrying out the project, with management retaining final approval power. However, on other teams, senior staff members may have a great deal of ownership and investment in the situation and may be able to assume the majority of the responsibility with guidance and support from management as necessary.

The team process model may require more time for planning because a conscious effort is made to involve staff at a maximum level. However, this time may be very well-spent. In addition to the formation of a comprehensive, targeted needs assessment, inclusion of staff can build momentum in the project and build staff support for a successful project.

A team process model calls for management to identify key staff members who are respected by their peers and who have good relational and communication skills. Usually an open invitation is made to all the staff so that any interested person has the opportunity to volunteer. Thus, staff members are included in the planning process, actively making decisions and serving as a liaison role between the rest of staff and management. They assist with specifying the problem through their own observations and experiences and are also able to obtain input from colleagues.

Although the team process model is not a pure "bottom-up" approach, it is a democratic one that relies solidly on staff to identify training needs as well as to shape the focus and process of the needs assessment. Most staff training needs assessments will retain an element of a "top-down" approach because the process requires management support and organizational resources for implementation. Case Example 2 (Supporting a Change in Practice) described earlier in this chapter illustrates the team process model in this context. The specific steps of the team process model when applied to a needs assessment are diagrammed in Figure 6.2.

Step Six: Data Collection

The collection of data is directly tied to the process and assessment methodology chosen for the project. (See Chapter 3 for more information concerning assessment content, sampling methods, and other specifics regarding this step of the needs assessment process.) Care should be taken to consider all of the elements previously reviewed to support the gathering of accurate data. The desired outcome of the data collection activity is to acquire the strongest data possible that is representative of the staff members for whom this problem affects. This will help ensure that training efforts driven by the data will be on target and will accurately address personnel or organizational deficits.

Step Seven: Data Analysis and Dissemination

The method chosen to analyze the data will depend on the type of data gathered in the needs assessment. Discussion of this issue, as well as other items and considerations related to data analysis, are covered in Chapter 4. When interpreting the data and preparing data for a report, it is important to remember the audience for whom you are writing and

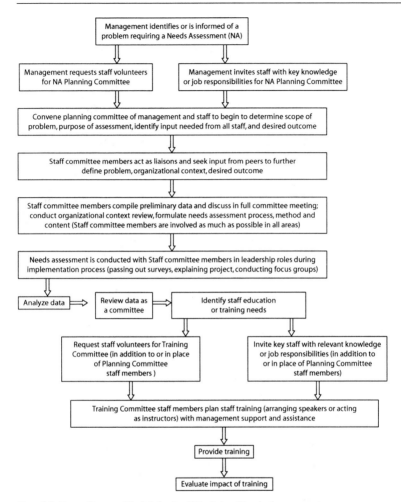

Figure 6.2 Team Process Model for Staff Training Needs Assessment

the purpose of the project so that the data are summarized and presented in a way that assists with staff training efforts. Because the data were obtained from staff, they must receive the findings and be considered part of the audience. This helps to keep the needs assessment process transparent and fosters their ownership and investment in the process.

Step Eight: Construct and Implement Training

Once the data have been analyzed and interpreted, the direction in which training efforts ought to proceed should be clear. If you recall the team process model, you will remember that staff involvement does not stop once the actual training needs are identified. Rather, whenever possible, maximum staff involvement is recommended to continue, albeit with a different focus. This is particularly important if the needs assessment uncovered professional training needs about which staff might be defensive if addressed by management alone.

For example, in one social service agency, the core function of a team of longstanding human service employees was going to be drastically changed because of reorganization. This shift in job responsibilities required a basic skill set that they had all been trained in but had not used for years because of the current focus of their work. Staff volunteers were asked to design both the content and the pedagogy (with management support) of training that would be used to help staff brush up on these little-used skills. This involvement of staff assisted the agency to present the training sessions in a way staff members could accept. It also reduced the odds that staff members might misinterpret management's motivation or intentions. This illustration of staff education highlights the importance of viewing administrators and staff members not as adversaries but as part of the same team, not only throughout the needs assessment process but in the provision of subsequent training as well.

Step Nine: Translating Learning to Practice and Evaluating Success

Both the needs assessment and the staff training share the goal of improving services within the organization. Translation of new learning into professional practice within the organizational structure requires planning, ongoing support, and evaluation of the effort. At this stage, the time spent involving and empowering staff has increased their buy-in and investment in the needs assessment and training process and should bring about a greater level of change. Staff members who have been part of the process are usually motivated to acquire new learning.

Example 3: Evaluating Training: Goals, Objectives, and Indicators

In Case Example 2, you may remember that the identified problem concerned the deficiency of supportive counseling to sexual assault patients seen in the medical trauma center. The following is an example of a goal, objective, and monitoring indicators that could be developed to address the staff needs assessment finding.

Goal: Increase supportive counseling provided by social workers to patients suffering from sexual assault.

Objective:
1. Staff deliver supportive counseling and document it in 100% of the sexual assault patients' charts the same day.

Monitoring indicators:
    a. Audit social worker documentation (activity checklist) and record percentage of tasks completed.
    b. Audit social worker documentation (narrative summary) for verification of the provision of supportive counseling intervention.
    c. Collect and review patient satisfaction data.

Monitoring the effectiveness of the training endeavor is more easily accomplished if training sessions are designed with clear, measurable goals and objectives at the onset. These goals and objectives can then be operationalized and used to craft indicators that can be used to evaluate the training. Indicators should be clearly defined and lend themselves to objective measurement of each area impacted by the training. It may be necessary to choose multiple indicators to fully monitor progress. Change is easier to assess if a baseline is obtained prior to training. Construction of goals, objectives, and monitoring indicators are illustrated in Example 3.

Review of data obtained after the training can lead to the conclusion that the deficit or need has been addressed and no further action is required. Conversely, evaluation efforts may identify a new problem or reveal that additional training is necessary to fully address the original need. These findings may indicate the need to begin the needs assessment process again. Indeed, Milner and Roberts (2002) present a model of educational and organizational needs assessment that supports this circular process.

Summary

In this chapter, we have presented an organization model that allows staff and administrators to work together in planning and implementing a staff training needs assessment. It is very likely that during a social worker's career there will be many opportunities to develop training needs assessments that could be helpful to social and human service agencies. There may also be times when a needs assessment is necessary, but on a scale much larger than a single agency. The next chapter will review an example of a needs assessment at a statewide macrolevel.

7

Conducting a Statewide
Needs Assessment

This chapter provides an example of a recently completed statewide needs assessment and applies many of the concepts introduced in previous chapters. In addition, some of the unique challenges of a statewide needs assessment are discussed. The goal of this chapter is to give the reader an example of a large-scale needs assessment study from start to finish. Specifically, the planning, data collection, and dissemination stages of a statewide substance abuse treatment needs assessment are described.

Planning

Purpose and Impact/Utility

As with all needs assessment studies, this example begins with a series of questions (see Chapter 2). The first question was to determine the purpose of the needs assessment and how the information would be used.

A few years ago, one of the authors was asked by the state agency in charge of substance abuse treatment services to conduct a large-scale needs assessment study. Each year, states receive federal money dedicated to substance abuse prevention and treatment services. The money comes in the form of a substance abuse prevention and treatment (SAPT) block grant from the Substance Abuse and Mental Health Services Administration. The amount of money a state receives is related to a variety of characteristics of the state, including the number of state residents who are in current need of substance abuse treatment. It had been a few years since statewide treatment need data had been collected in Kentucky. The primary goal of the needs assessment study, therefore, was to provide an updated estimate of the number of Kentuckians who needed but were not receiving substance abuse treatment. In other words, this needs assessment focused on service need rather than availability, accessibility, or acceptability of services (see Chapter 1).

The state agency was most interested in obtaining two sets of estimates of substance abuse treatment need. First and foremost, a state-level estimate of treatment need was needed so that Kentucky could provide the information necessary to receive its annual SAPT block grant. These updated estimates would also provide information about how substance abuse treatment had changed since the last statewide needs assessment. Second, the state was interested in obtaining substance abuse treatment need at the county level. The state of Kentucky has 120 counties. Many residents, particularly rural residents, identify with their county more than their particular town. Most of the health and social services, as well as the public schools, are administered at the county level. Furthermore, county-level data would provide counties with a sense of what their substance abuse treatment needs are and how they compare to surrounding counties. For these and other reasons, the state had interest in obtaining county-level data. The state agency provided financial support and a 15-month time-frame to complete the project.

Assembling the Team

Once the purpose, time, and available resources for conducting the needs assessment study were determined, assembling the research team became the next step in the planning process. A six-person multidisciplinary team was assembled, and each member brought a different set of skills and experiences to the research table. One team member was a social worker who had expertise in substance abuse research and policy at the national level. Another team member was a sociologist who had experience in designing surveys and examining population-based research questions. A third team member had clinical experience working with substance abuse treatment clients and graduate training in epidemiology. Another team member had experience as a substance abuse treatment program administrator in Kentucky. One team member was a psychologist with expertise in methodology and data analysis. Finally, a graduate student research assistant was included on the team.

The team met several times a month to plan the needs assessment study and to define individual roles and responsibilities, including time commitments, for completing the study. We decided to organize the needs assessment study activities under the name Kentucky Needs Assessment Project (KNAP). One of us served as the scientific leader, or principal investigator, and oversaw all aspects of the project. The principal investigator was responsible for ensuring that the resources were effectively used and that project goals were achieved. Another team member acted as the study director and made major contributions to writing and data analysis. A third team member focused on designing the study sample and instrumentation. Two members served in an advisory (and voluntary) capacity and agreed to review drafts of instrumentation and the final needs assessment report. Finally, the graduate level assistant helped the team with compiling the relevant research literature and producing all KNAP documentation, including the final project report.

One of our first orders of business was to create a project timeline. The process of creating a timeline helped the team think through the tasks that needed to be completed, the order in which they should be completed, and the length of time it would take to complete them. The KNAP timeline can be seen in Figure 7.1.

Deciding on the Approach

So, with our team assembled, we began discussions about how best to achieve the goals of the needs assessment study with the available time and resources provided by the state agency funding the project.

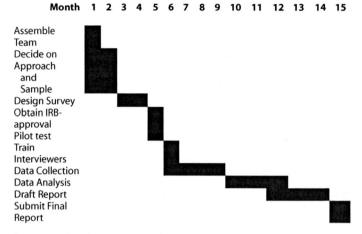

Figure 7.1 Kentucky Needs Assessment Project Timeline

Large-scale needs assessment studies have various characteristics, which may differ from other needs assessment studies. Perhaps most important is that estimates of need are provided rather than actual need. To do a needs assessment of a daycare center or local neighborhood, it may be realistic to obtain information on every individual, assess their individual need, and then simply add up the number of people who had a particular need to arrive at a final number. Although this method returns an exact number of persons in need, it is not always a practical approach, particularly for a statewide assessment of individual-level needs.

For example, the adult state population of Kentucky was 3.1 million at the time this particular KNAP study was conducted. To obtain the most accurate count of individual substance abuse treatment need, we could have performed an assessment on every one of the 3.1 million adult residents. Assuming 20 minutes per individual assessment, 62 million minutes of data collection would be required to obtain individual-level data on each adult Kentuckian. In other words, each of the six team members would have to perform assessments on individuals non-stop for nearly 20 years! Aside from the fact that such a study would be astronomically expensive and a logistical nightmare to conduct, this approach would likely fail to provide exact results because, in the time it would take to collect the data, the statewide substance abuse treatment needs are likely to change because of shifts in culture, population, and economic conditions.

Researchers conducting large-scale needs assessment, therefore, often turn to estimation methods to determine the level of need in the population. Specifically, data are collected from a smaller sample of individuals and then analyzed to determine what percentage of individuals are in need of the particular service being examined—in our case, substance abuse treatment. The percentage of individuals in need from the smaller sample is then applied to the larger population to estimate the number of individuals who are in need. Needless to say, the research team quickly agreed that an estimation method was the only viable option to determine the statewide substance abuse treatment need. We knew we would have to collect data from a random and representative sample of adult Kentuckians to arrive at reliable estimates of substance abuse treatment need. Our next step was to formally define the sample from which we would collect data.

Defining the Sample

The primary goal of the needs assessment study was to estimate the number of adult Kentuckians who needed but were not receiving substance abuse treatment. First, we needed to decide whom to include in our sample. We created a list of inclusion, or eligibility, criteria. Because the goal was to estimate the substance abuse treatment needs of adults, we excluded any person younger than 18 years old. We also decided that only residents of Kentucky should be included in the sample. A more complicated decision was our choice to include only adult Kentuckians who lived in residential households, thus eliminating individuals who were homeless, incarcerated, or resided in group-living situations (e.g., dormitories or nursing homes). The decision to include only adults living in residential households was made for two reasons. First, we found a strong precedent in the research literature for sampling only households when conducting large-scale studies such as KNAP. Second, there are myriad challenges in accessing populations with other living conditions, and it creates the possibility that a person might be sampled more than once (e.g., once while living at home, once in jail). That said, we understood that not including these other groups would be a limitation of the study that we would have to clearly state in our final project report.

After deciding who should be in the sample, we then had to decide how many people should be in the sample. Many factors came into play in this decision. The amount of time and resources available were one set of factors. The method of data collection (described later) was another. A third factor was how precise we wanted to make our estimates of substance abuse treatment need.

The precision of the estimates, or the degree to which the estimates are likely to be close to the true number of persons in need, depends on three related characteristics of the sample on which the estimate is based. First, the sample used to calculate the percentage of need should be a random sample. In other words, every person in the population being studied should have an equal chance of being selected as a study participant (see Chapter 3).

Second, the sample should be representative of the larger population for which the need is being estimated. If the sample is not representative of the population of the group being studied, generalizations to that population cannot be made. Imagine, for example, if we decided to collect data for KNAP by interviewing the first 10 customers at the neighborhood liquor store on four consecutive Monday mornings. Chances are that a different level of substance abuse treatment need would be found in this sample than in a truly random and representative sample of adult Kentuckians. Or, what if we had randomly sampled only residents of the local city because they were easier to access than a statewide sample? We would be able to generalize our findings to the city, but probably not the rest of the state where the demographic characteristics (e.g., socio-economic status, education level, and race) vary from one geographic region to another.

Finally, the sample should be large enough to reduce the margin of error of the estimates. If the sample is a random and representative sample, then the precision of the survey estimates increases as the sample size increases, and consequently, the margin of error decreases. Another way to think about the margin of error is to think about how much confidence one wants to have that the estimates reflect the true number of persons in need (for more information on margin of error, *see* http://www.whatisasurvey.info/).

Recall that the state agency was interested in obtaining estimates of substance abuse treatment need at both the state and the county level. To get reliable estimates of substance abuse treatment need at the county level, we calculated that several hundred individuals, selected at random, would need to be interviewed from each county. Remembering that there are 120 counties in Kentucky, tens of thousands of interviews would need to be completed to provide reasonably reliable estimates!

Because resources would not allow us to provide reliable estimates at the county level, we arrived at a compromise to investigate substance abuse treatment needs at a regional level. Kentucky substance abuse treatment services are administered throughout Kentucky's 14 Mental Health and Mental Retardation (MHMR) regions. Each MHMR region is comprised of a cluster of contiguous counties, each county belonging to only one MHMR region. These MHMR regions, therefore, are meaningful geographic regions, and estimates based on this level were likely to provide more utility for the state agency than if we had created state regions arbitrarily.

To provide reliable estimates at both the state and MHMR levels, we decided our sample should be a random stratified sample. In other words, rather than randomly sampling the entire state, we decided to randomly sample each MHMR region independently so that the number of respondents and the margin of error of the estimates were comparable across regions. Based on this sampling design and available resources, we agreed to aim for a minimum of 286 survey respondents per MHMR region, which resulted in a margin of error of no more than ±5.75% for estimates made at the MHMR level.

Deciding on a Data Collection Method

There are ever-increasing ways to collect data from individuals, each with its own set of pros and cons. Mailed surveys are attractive to researchers because, for the price of a stamp, many people across many miles can be contacted. Mail surveys, however, have relatively low return rates and a variety of data quality concerns can arise. For example, there is little control over who actually completes the survey, no way to provide clarification for a respondent if there is confusion about the survey or any particular survey item, and certain populations can be removed inadvertently from the sample (e.g., persons with blindness or illiteracy). Therefore, we decided against a mail survey.

As computer technology has become more advanced and widespread, so have the electronic methods to collect data. Similar to the mail survey, E-mail and Internet surveys are increasingly being used to collect data from individuals. These methods can be even less costly than mail surveys (no stamp!) but suffer from most of the same problems of mail surveys. For example, not all state residents have ready access to the Internet or are even computer-literate.

In-person interviewing was also considered briefly for the needs assessment study. The National Survey on Drug Use and Health (NSDUH; http://oas.samhsa.gov/nsduh.htm), which is the major substance use survey used to determine rates of alcohol and drug use across the country, uses in-person interviewer methodology. Specifically, a computer-assisted personal interviewing (CAPI) methodology is used, whereby an interviewer visits a randomly selected home and interviews one or two residents with the assistance of a preprogrammed laptop that guides the interview and allows for on-the-spot data entry. Although this option has many merits, its major weaknesses (cost and time) eliminated it as a potential data collection approach for our needs assessment study.

Although we were unable to use the methodology from the NSDUH in conducting our own survey, we did consider using NSDUH data to address our question of substance abuse treatment need in Kentucky. The use of secondary data has several strengths (see Chapter 3). First, we would be able to benefit from the CAPI methodology without actually incurring its associated costs. Considerable time would be saved as well. Furthermore, the NSDUH has data available for individual states, which would allow us to compare (*benchmark*) the substance abuse treatment need in Kentucky to the need found in other states using the same data collection method. In the end, one major disadvantage led us away from using the NSDUH as our major data source. As previously mentioned, we wanted to be able to compare substance abuse treatment need across the 14 MHMR regions. To accomplish this, we needed a random sample stratified by MHMR region with an adequate number of respondents per MHMR region to allow for reliable estimates. At the time, the most current NSDUH data included only 602 adults in its Kentucky sample, and the sampling plan was not based on MHMR region. Even if data had been collected from an equal number of respondents from each MHMR region, the individual MHMR region estimates would be based on 43 responses, with a margin of error more than ±15%.

The final approach we considered for the collection of needs assessment data was through telephone surveys. Telephone surveys have many of the strengths of the in-person interviews but suffer from some of the weaknesses of other survey approaches. In addition, telephone surveys have some advantages over in-person interviews (McAuliffe et al., 1998). In a large-scale survey, telephone surveys tend to have lower costs, more opportunity to monitor interviewers as they collect data, and greater security and privacy, and they can be easier to administer. Telephone surveys also can provide a greater sense of anonymity for respondents, which is important when the topic matter is sensitive, such as substance use and treatment needs. For these reasons, we chose to use a telephone survey approach.

Given the scope of a statewide needs assessment, it was determined that the team would need the assistance of an organization with the requisite experience and infrastructure to perform several thousand telephone calls. We contacted the local university survey research center, which agreed to a subcontract to collect data. There are several benefits to using a survey research center. First, survey research centers already have trained interviewing staff members who have administered dozens of surveys; therefore, only a brief training is required to acclimate interviewers to a new survey. Second, university or similar research centers have experience with drawing samples from banks of telephone numbers and can tailor this activity to the needs of a particular survey. Perhaps most importantly, larger survey research centers have a computer-assisted

1. Have specific goals.
2. Consider alternatives.
3. Select samples that well represent the population to be studied.
4. Use designs that balance costs with errors.
5. Take great care in matching question wording to the concepts being measured and the population studied.
6. Pretest questionnaires and procedures.
7. Train interviewers carefully on interviewing techniques and the subject matter of the survey.
8. Check quality at each stage.
9. Maximize cooperation or response rates within the limits of ethical treatment of human subjects.
10. Use appropriate statistical analytic and reporting techniques.
11. Develop and fulfill pledges of confidentiality given to respondents.
12. Disclose all methods of the survey to allow for evaluation and replication.

Source: Best Practices for Survey and Public Opinion Research, American Association for Public Opinion Research

Figure 7.2   Best Practices for Survey Research

telephone interview (CATI) system, which allows for efficient and reliable data collection. Additional benefits of the CATI system are discussed later in the section on data collection. For further discussion of data collection methods in the context of time, resources, and expertise, see Chapter 3.

Survey Construction

The research team was fortunate in that the federal government had a substance abuse treatment needs assessment survey that had been used in other states, including Kentucky, and could be used as a model. We were also able to find a wealth of information on standards for conducting survey research (see Figure 7.2).

Because the state agency was interested in current substance use and treatment need and how it had changed over time, many of the questions from the survey previously used in Kentucky were retained so that a direct comparison between the two surveys (1999 vs. 2004) could be made. The survey was also modified in several ways. In the few years prior to the needs assessment study, two new drugs emerged as major problems in Kentucky. The first, OxyContin, had been in the news frequently, and stories often focused on the high rates of addiction to this prescription painkiller in the eastern, Appalachian area of the state. The second drug, methamphetamine, was becoming more and more of a problem in the western part of the state. To capture information on these substances, new questions were added to the survey instrument.

Care was taken to make sure that all of our needs assessment questions could be answered with the survey questions. Most importantly, we had to make sure we had items to measure substance abuse treatment need. Other questions were removed if they did not have relevance to the primary goal of KNAP. The final version of the survey contained a total of 270 possible questions; however, few—if any—respondents were asked all the questions because many of them were asked only if the respondent answered a preceding question in a certain way. For example, if a respondent answered that she had never consumed alcohol, she was not asked follow-up questions about how many days she used alcohol in the past 30 days or about problems associated with her alcohol use.

Another consideration was the potential that we may reach residences in which there were no English-speaking individuals. After consulting state-level information on other major languages spoken in the state, it was determined that Spanish was the most likely non-English language we would encounter. To address this potential language barrier, we worked with two Spanish-speaking translators to adapt the survey to Spanish. The first translator worked with the English version of the survey and translated it into Spanish. The second translator took the Spanish-translated version of the survey and back-translated it into English. These activities were performed independently. The needs assessment team and the translators met to work through the few discrepancies between the original English version and the back-translated version. These discrepancies were primarily a result of nuances of the Spanish language and were easily resolved.

Institutional Review Board Approval

Because the KNAP was a research study involving data collection from human participants, the survey and research methodology had to be approved by an IRB (see Chapter 2). In fact, in our case, two separate IRBs had to review the project—one at the university and one at state government. Institutional review boards serve the important function of ensuring that proper safeguards are in place to protect human subjects from being harmed as a result of their participation in a research study. These committees review, approve, and monitor all research protocol involving human participants, as well as other types of research. The U. S. Department of Health and Human Services provides important information regarding the protection of human subjects, which IRBs and researchers must follow (http://www.hhs.gov/ohrp/humansubjects/guidance/45cfr46.htm).

Data Collection

Training and Pilot Testing

At the beginning of the study, interviewers were required to attend a 4-hour project orientation with members of the needs assessment research team, during which goals of the study were introduced and survey questions were read aloud and discussed. After this general introduction, interviewer pairs conducted mock interviews with one another until each had a chance to complete the entire interview. Once all interviewers were comfortable with the survey questions, the interview was pilot-tested with several respondents to identify potential problems with the survey instrument.

Administering the Survey

With the interviewers acclimated to the survey and the remaining problems resolved, data collection commenced. During the first few weeks of interviews, interviewers were closely monitored. Extra supervisors were staffed during the initial calling shifts to help provide monitoring until all interviewers completed several interviews. Then, throughout data collection, supervisors periodically listened on a third, "quiet line," for quality control.

As mentioned earlier, the survey was administered through the use of a CATI system at the university survey research center. The CATI system had more than two dozen computer workstations from which interviews could be conducted simultaneously. The computer randomly selected a phone number from a prescreened list and presented it to the interviewer to dial. This process is called the random-digit dialing method and ensures that every residential phone, listed or unlisted, has an equal probability of being selected.

Another benefit of the CATI system was that the data were entered at the time of the interview, allowing for constant monitoring of productivity and quality. Data were reviewed by the survey research center on a weekly basis to monitor interview length and abnormal response patterns. In addition, the CATI logged all attempted calls and provided an automatic scheduling algorithm, which ensured that phone numbers were attempted at different hours on different days until contact was made.

To maximize participation among eligible potential subjects, procedures were used to enhance cooperation. Interviewers were trained to be sensitive to the concerns of respondents about the study goals. Up to 15 call attempts were made to each phone number. In addition, up to 10 scheduled callbacks were made to those reached at an inconvenient time. Eligible respondents who indicated that they were not interested in participating were called an additional time. Callbacks often result in "conversions" from initial refusals to willing participants. If an eligible respondent refused a second time, the household was not contacted again.

Once a household was contacted, it was screened to determine if any residents met the eligibility criteria. In situations where more than one member of the household was eligible, the respondent was randomly selected from all eligible residents by asking to speak with the adult who had the most recent birthday. This "last-birthday" algorithm helped ensure random selection within the household. If necessary, a callback was arranged.

After the household was screened for eligibility, the study was explained to each respondent and verbal consent was obtained before questions were asked. Maintaining confidentiality was stressed to protect the respondent's right to privacy and to assure data quality. If the interviewer was not certain the conversation could be conducted in private, then the interview was terminated and the data discarded.

Data collection took approximately 4 months. The university survey research center supplied the research team with a data set as well as information about the disposition of calls, which included the number of telephone contacts, incligible households, refusals, and the response rate. Approximately 12,800 different telephone numbers were contacted to complete 4,200 interviews. Five of these interviews were judged to be of low quality by the person conducting the interview and were discarded. The survey research center also supplied a list of 22 phone numbers that were answered by a Spanish-speaking person. One of the translators called these telephone numbers and was able to complete an additional 15 interviews. The final sample available for analysis consisted of 4210 adult Kentuckians.

The overall *response rate* for the telephone survey was 34.0%. The response rate was calculated by taking the total number of completed interviews and dividing them by the total number of contacted households that were eligible for the study. In this case, the 4200 completed interviews by the survey research center and the 15 completed interviews by the translator were divided by the number of contacted households minus the 418 ineligible households:

$$\text{Response Rate} = \frac{(4200 + 15) \text{ completed interviews}}{(12{,}822 \text{ contacted households} - 418 \text{ ineligible})} = 34.0\%$$

It is important not to confuse the response rate with other related terms such as the *cooperation rate* (the proportion of all households interviewed of all eligible households contacted), the *refusal rate* (the proportion of all households in which a potentially eligible respondent refused to be interviewed or terminated an interview), and *contact rate* (the proportion of all households in which some household member was reached). Additional information on response, cooperation, refusal, and contact rates, as well as a useful response rate calculator, can be found on The American Association for Public Opinion Research Web site at www.aapor.org.

Data Analysis

The first step in data analysis was to check that each of the variables contained legitimate values. Specifically, numerous descriptive statistics were used to gain an understanding of the characteristics of each of the survey items. Frequencies, ranges, means, medians, and modes were examined for each variable (*see* Chapter 4). Next, general demographic variables were analyzed to determine the extent to which the random sample represented the overall state population. Although we had a large sample of survey respondents, we found differences in age, gender, and MHMR region in the sample, and therefore, standard data weights were developed to statistically adjust the sample to be more representative of the state's population. In other words, the responses from survey respondents who were known to be under-represented in the sample (e.g., young males) were counted more toward the overall average on each individual survey item (e.g., lifetime alcohol use) than responses from individuals who were either appropriately represented or over-represented in the sample (e.g., older females). Most statistical software packages have a data weight option that can apply these statistical adjustments.

With this newly created weighted data set, we then began to systematically analyze each of the variables. During data collection, we outlined the sections of the final report and the information to be included in each section. We also used this outline as a way to structure our analyses. Two team members, the principal investigator and the study director, conducted the analyses and made data-coding decisions.

Interpreting Data

Once the analyses were performed, preliminary data tables were constructed and discussed in team meetings. Special attention was given to unexpected results and what might account for them. Suggestions for additional analyses were made. Another important step was interpreting the data in the context of other available data sources. For example, we were interested if the study results were consistent with other similar studies. For the KNAP study, two national studies were relevant.

The previously mentioned NSDUH study and the National Co-Morbidity Study Replication (NCS-R) both collect information on drug use and information about treatment. Although the methodologies are different, these studies examine similar issues and are well known. The KNAP findings for substance abuse treatment need were not as high as the NSDUH (Office of Applied Studies, 2003) but not as low as the NCS-R (Kessler et al., 2005). We also compared the data to previous needs assessment estimates for the state of Kentucky. Differences between the KNAP project and earlier studies were similar to the substance use changes seen at the national level over the same time-period. These findings gave us additional confidence in the results of the KNAP study.

Dissemination

The Audience

After data were analyzed, we turned our attention to disseminating the results of the KNAP study (see Chapter 5). We prepared to make the information available and useful to a variety of audiences. First and foremost, we had to disseminate the study results to the state agency that funded the project. However, given the widespread problem of substance abuse and the interest in reducing it, we were aware that other audiences would likely be interested in the KNAP study. We anticipated secondary audiences might be policymakers, treatment providers, prevention specialists, criminal justice professionals, researchers, and concerned citizens. Because a diverse audience was going to consume the research findings, we made a concerted effort to minimize the use of scientific jargon and to avoid presenting complex statistical analyses. Instead, the only statistics we decided to present were percentages and averages.

Writing the Report

At the beginning of the KNAP study we agreed to write a project report to be delivered to the state agency that funded the needs assessment

1. The sponsorship of the study.
2. A description of the purposes.
3. The sample description and size.
4. The dates of data collection.
5. The names of the researchers or organization conducting the study.
6. The exact wording of the questions.
7. Additional information a lay person would need to make a reasonable assessment of the reported findings.

Source: Responsibilities in Reporting to Clients and the Public, Council of American Survey Research Organizations

Figure 7.3 Minimum Guidelines for Reporting Survey Results to the Public

study. Because the state agency planned on sharing the results of the study with other community and government organizations, the report was written for a wide audience. We consulted other information sources to determine if there were any guidelines on what information should be included in the KNAP report. We found a variety of professional survey associations that provided guidelines for the dissemination of survey research findings (see Figure 7.3 and list at the end of this chapter).

The writing of the report followed the process described in Chapter 5. The research team members in charge of writing the report drafted the first few sections and distributed them to other team members for feedback. Formatting changes and the presentation of the data were discussed. The initial sections were revised accordingly, and the remaining sections were written and distributed for internal review by KNAP team members.

The KNAP report was divided into:

- An Executive Summary
- Purpose and Objectives
- Methods
- Data Analysis and Findings
- Conclusions
- References
- Appendix containing the survey instrument

Presentation of Findings

Data were presented in a variety of ways. When we wanted to display several pieces of data at once, we found constructing tables to be the most effective. This method also allowed for stratification of data so that readers could see how two subgroups compared across several variables. Table 7.1 presents the KNAP stimulant use data, stratified by gender.

Other data were presented in graphical form. Bar charts, line graphs, and pie charts were used to present gender differences with respect to their use of more prevalent substances such as alcohol (see Figure 7.4). This type of data presentation was particularly effective for highlighting large differences between groups.

Because the KNAP study used a random stratified sample design, we were also able to present data at the MHMR level to show geographic variations in variables of interest. We found that data maps were a very effective way to present these data. Although this form of data presentation requires slightly more effort, data maps from the KNAP study have been well-received and require minimal explanation. Adult Kentuckian substance abuse treatment need by MHMR Region is shown in Figure 7.5.[A]

The Limitations

Because the audience of the needs assessment study was quite diverse, it was important to clearly state the limitations of the research. First, we discussed limitations of the sample. In this needs assessment study, only adults living in residential households were interviewed; therefore, the

---

A Adult Kentuckians were considered in need of substance abuse treatment if they met any of the following criteria: (1) a self-report of needing but not receiving substance abuse treatment; (2) meeting the DSM-IV-TR criteria for substance abuse or dependence in the past 12 months; (3) continued use of substances in the past 12 months despite self-reported problems related to substance use; (4) engaging in high-risk behavior related to substance use in the past 12 months; or (5) using substances in the past 30 days and current pregnancy. Note that these criteria represent both *felt need* and *comparative need* (see Chapter 1).

Table 7.1 Estimated Number of Adult Kentuckians Who Ever Used
Stimulants

	Males	Females	Total
Cocaine	150,663	78,568	229,231
Methamphetamines	60,859	20,744	81,603
Ecstasy	40,078	29,635	69,713
Other Stimulants	151,405	70,414	221,819

estimates for treatment need can be generalized only to this population.
It was likely that the substance use and treatment needs differed for other
populations such as those who were less than 18 years old, homeless, or
incarcerated. Second, because the data were self-reported, the validity of
the data depended on the honesty, memory, and understanding of the
respondents. We also were limited by the fact some households did not
have telephones and were therefore eliminated from the sample.

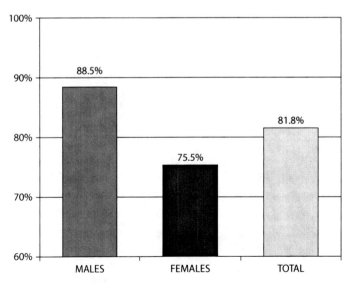

Figure 7.4 Percent of Adult Kentuckians Who Drank at Least One Alcoholic
Beverage in Their Life

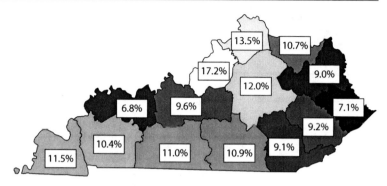

Figure 7.5 Estimated Percentage of Adult Kentuckians in Need of Substance Abuse Treatment by MHMR Region

Delivering the Report

Once the report had undergone several internal drafts and reviews by the needs assessment team, a draft copy was sent to the state agency for review. Two team members met with the state agency director to review the contents of the report and answered any questions. Once it was clear that the report was acceptable, dozens of bound copies of the report were provided for the state agency to distribute at their discretion. The report was also placed on the Internet for further dissemination (a copy of the final KNAP report and survey instrument can be downloaded at http://cdar.uky.edu/knap).

Dissemination

The final task on the KNAP timeline was submitting the final project report. However, we learned that although this was the formal ending of the project, our work with the needs assessment survey continued well beyond the official end date. Once the study results were disseminated, we received requests from a variety of individuals and groups for more information about the needs assessment study. Lobbyists called to obtain substance abuse treatment need data for certain regions of state, researchers contacted us for preliminary data to be used in grant applications, organizations asked us to give presentations, the funding agency asked for more bound copies of the final report, and several media requests for interviews were entertained. We were even asked to write a book chapter on conducting a statewide needs assessment.

Summary

This chapter has provided an applied example of an actual needs assessment conducted at the state level by a multidisciplinary research team. The chapter illustrated the various steps outlined earlier in the book and explained many of the processes and decisions that were made in the planning, data collection, and dissemination stages of the needs assessment. Conducting a large-scale needs assessment involves much greater coordination than smaller scale efforts, and therefore, careful planning is essential to successfully completing a needs assessment with a scope as large as the one described in this chapter. Finally, we presented several ways to present and disseminate the results of a needs assessment study so that the information can reach a variety of audiences.

Survey-Related Professional Organizations

- American Association for Public Opinion Research (www.aapor.org)
- American Statistical Association (www.amstat.org)
- Council of American Survey Research Organizations (www.casro.org)
- National Council on Public Polls (www.ncpp.org)
- World Association for Public Opinion Research (www.wapor.org)

Appendix

Survey of Program Training Needs (TCU PTN)
Staff Version (TCU PTN-S)

To be completed by <u>Clinical Supervisor</u> and <u>Clinical Staff</u>

Please answer the following questions by filling in the circle that describes your substance abuse program. For the purpose of this survey, a "program" refers to a <u>single</u> treatment modality (e.g., outpatient or therapeutic community) at a <u>single</u> site delivered by a designated staff.

Are you: O *Male*   O *Female*   Your Birth Year: 19|___|___|

Are you Hispanic or Latino?   O *No*   O *Yes*

Are you: [MARK ONE]
O *American Indian/Alaska Native*
O *Asian*
O *Native Hawaiian or Other Pacific Islander*
O *Black or African American*

O *White*
O *More than one race*
O *Other* (specify): _____

---

1. Today's Date: .... |___|___||___|___||___|___|
                                                               MO   DAY   YR

2. Zip code of program: .... |___|___|___|___|___|

3. Are you the clinical supervisor for this program? .... O Yes   O No

	Number of Years						
	1	2	3	4	5	6	7	8+

4. Background:

Years you have worked –

a. in the drug treatment <u>field</u>? .... O   O   O   O   O   O   O   O

b. at this <u>program</u>? .... O   O   O   O   O   O   O   O

c. in your current <u>position</u>? .... O   O   O   O   O   O   O   O

	Disagree Strongly (1)	Disagree (2)	Uncertain (3)	Agree (4)	Agree Strongly (5)

How strongly do you agree or disagree with each of the following statements?

Facilities and Climate

5. Offices, equipment, and supplies are adequate at your program. .... ○ ○ ○ ○ ○

6. Your program has enough counselors and staff to meet current client needs. ...... ○ ○ ○ ○ ○

7. Your program has adequate resources for meeting most medical and psychiatric client needs. .... ○ ○ ○ ○ ○

8. Most program staff feel positive and confident about the quality of services at your program. .... ○ ○ ○ ○ ○

9. Your program has a secure future ahead. .... ○ ○ ○ ○ ○

10. Program staff here get along very well. .... ○ ○ ○ ○ ○

11. Program staff morale is very good. .... ○ ○ ○ ○ ○

Satisfaction with Training

12. Good in-house (inservice) training is provided to program staff. .... ○ ○ ○ ○ ○

13. You found good outside training events to attend last year. .... ○ ○ ○ ○ ○

14. Your state-funded drug or alcohol agency provided good training in the past year. .... ○ ○ ○ ○ ○

15. Regional authorities or groups (e.g., ATTC, ACA) provided good training in the past year. .... ○ ○ ○ ○ ○

Training Content Preferences	Disagree Strongly (1)	Disagree (2)	Uncertain (3)	Agree (4)	Agree Strongly (5)
16. You want more scientific information on the neurobiology of addiction.	O	O	O	O	O
17. More pharmacotherapy information and training are needed on new medications.	O	O	O	O	O
18. Program staff need sensitivity training for dealing with special populations.	O	O	O	O	O
19. Program staff training is needed on ethics and confidentiality of information.	O	O	O	O	O
20. Specialized training is needed for improving family involvement and related issues.	O	O	O	O	O
21. Program staff training is needed on dual diagnoses and appropriate treatment.	O	O	O	O	O
22. Training to use brief diagnostic screening tools would be helpful to program staff.	O	O	O	O	O
23. Program staff need to be trained to understand other staff functions (e.g., correctional officer duties).	O	O	O	O	O

Counseling staff needs more training for –

	Disagree Strongly (1)	Disagree (2)	Uncertain (3)	Agree (4)	Agree Strongly (5)
24. assessing client problems and needs.	O	O	O	O	O
25. increasing client participation in treatment.	O	O	O	O	O
26. monitoring client progress.	O	O	O	O	O
27. improving rapport with clients.	O	O	O	O	O
28. improving client thinking skills.	O	O	O	O	O
29. improving client problem-solving skills.	O	O	O	O	O
30. improving behavioral management of clients.	O	O	O	O	O
31. improving cognitive focus of clients during group counseling.	O	O	O	O	O

FOR ADMINISTRATIVE PURPOSES

	Disagree Strongly (1)	Disagree (2)	Uncertain (3)	Agree (4)	Agree Strongly (5)
32. using computerized client assessments.	O	O	O	O	O
33. working with staff in other units/agencies.	O	O	O	O	O

Training Strategy Preferences

34. General introductory sessions on multiple topics is an effective workshop format.	O	O	O	O	O
35. Intensive full-day training on special topics is an effective workshop format.	O	O	O	O	O
36. A conceptual treatment process model documenting how treatment activities contribute to "recovery" would be helpful.	O	O	O	O	O
37. Training workshops should be based on evidence-based interventions.	O	O	O	O	O
38. Training workshops should be based on manual-guided interventions.	O	O	O	O	O
39. Training workshops should include role playing and group activities.	O	O	O	O	O
40. Telephone consultations following specialized training would be useful.	O	O	O	O	O
41. Specialized training made available over the Internet would be useful.	O	O	O	O	O
42. Exchanging ideas with other programs that have interests similar to yours would be helpful.	O	O	O	O	O
43. On-site consultation following training would be helpful.	O	O	O	O	O

Computer Resources

44. Most client records for this program are computerized.	O	O	O	O	O
45. Program staff here feel comfortable using computers.	O	O	O	O	O

	Disagree Strongly (1)	Disagree (2)	Uncertain (3)	Agree (4)	Agree Strongly (5)
46. More computer resources are needed here.	O	O	O	O	O
47. Program staff here have easy access for using e-mail and the Internet at work.	O	O	O	O	O
48. This program has policies that limit program staff access to the Internet and use of e-mail.	O	O	O	O	O

Barriers to Training

49. The workload and pressures at this program keep motivation for new training low.	O	O	O	O	O
50. The budget does not allow most program staff to attend professional conferences annually.	O	O	O	O	O
51. Topics presented at recent training workshops and conferences have been too limited.	O	O	O	O	O
52. The quality of trainers at recent workshops and conferences has been poor.	O	O	O	O	O
53. Training activities take too much time away from delivery of program services.	O	O	O	O	O
54. Training interests of program staff are mostly due to licensure or certification requirements.	O	O	O	O	O
55. It is often too difficult to adapt things learned at workshops so they will work in this program.	O	O	O	O	O
56. Limited resources (e.g., office space or budget) make it difficult to adopt new treatment ideas.	O	O	O	O	O
57. The background and training of program staff limits the kind of treatment changes possible here.	O	O	O	O	O
58. There are too few rewards for trying to change treatment or other procedures here.	O	O	O	O	O

References

Acosta, O., & Toro, P. A. (2000). Let's ask the homeless people themselves: A needs assessment based on a probability sample of adults. *American Journal of Community Psychology*, 28(3), 343–366.

Aviles, A. & Helfrich, C. (2004). Life skill service needs: Perspectives of homeless youth. *Journal of Youth and Adolescence*, 33 (4), 331–338.

Batsche, C., Hernandez, M. & Montenegro, M. C. (1999). Community needs assessment with Hispanic, Spanish-monolingual residents. *Evaluation and Program Planning*, 22, 13–20.

Berg, B. (1998). *Qualitative research methods for the social sciences*. 3rd Edition. Boston: Allyn & Bacon.

Best, D., Day, E. & Campbell, A. (2007). Developing a method for conducting needs assessment for drug treatment: A systems approach. *Addiction Research & Theory*, 15 (3), 263–275.

Beverly, C.J., Mcatee, R., Costello, J., Chernoff, R., & Casteel, J. (2005). Needs assessment of rural communities: A focus on older adults. *Journal of Community Health*, 30(3), 197–212.

Bradshaw, J. (1977). The concept of social need. In N. Gilbert & H. Specht, (Eds.), *Planning for social welfare: Issues, models and tasks*. Englewood Cliffs, NJ: Prentice Hall.

Brody, R. (2005). *Effectively managing human services organizations*. Thousand Oaks, CA: Sage Publications.

Cassidy, E.L., et al. (2005). Assessment to intervention: utilizing a staff needs assessment to improve care for behaviorally challenging residents in long term care (Part II). *Clinical Gerontologist*, 29(1), 27–38.

Chrislip, D. D. (2002). *The collaborative leadership fieldbook*. San Francisco, CA: Jossey Bass.

Cook, G.M. & Oei, T.S. (1998). A review of systematic and quantifiable methods of estimating the needs of a community for alcohol treatment services. *Journal of Substance Abuse Treatment*, 15 (4), 357–365.

Courtney, K.O., Joe, G.W., Rowan-Szal, & Simpson, D. (2007). Using organizational assessment as a tool for program change, *Journal of Substance Abuse Treatment*, 23, 131-137.

Daiski, I. (2007). Perspectives of homeless people on their health and health needs priorities. *Journal of Advanced Nursing*, 58(3), 273–281.

Ernst, J. S. (2000). Mapping child maltreatment: Looking at neighborhoods in a suburb an county. *Child Welfare*, 70, 555–572.

Ensign, J. (2003). Ethical issues in qualitative health research with homeless youths. *Journal of Advanced Nursing*, 43 (1), 43–50.

Gfroerer, J., Epstein, J., & Wright, D. (2004). Estimating substance abuse treatment need by state. *Addiction*, 99 (8), 938–939.

Hampton, C. & Vilela, M. (2007). Conducting surveys. The Community Tool Box. Retrieved November 12, 2007 from ctb.ky.edu.

Hillier, A. (2007). Why social work needs mapping. *Journal of Social Work Education*, 43 (2), 205–221.

Johnson, T. P., Hougland, J. G., & Clayton, R. R. (1989). Obtaining reports of sensitive behavior: A comparison of substance use reports from telephone and face-to-face interviews. *Social Science Quarterly*, 70(1), 174–183.

Kessler, R. C., Berglund, P., Demler, O., Jin, R., Merikangas, K. R., & Walters, E. E. (2005). Lifetime prevalence and age-of-onset distributions of DSM-IV disorders in the National Comorbidity Survey Replication. *Archives of General Psychiatry*, 62, 593–602.

Kramer, R., et al. (2002). Community needs assessment of lower Manhattan residents from the World Trade Center attacks—Manhattan, New York City, 2001. Centers for Disease Control, *MMWR Weekly*, 51, 10–13.

Lewis, M.J., West, B., Bautista, L., Greenberg, A.M., & Done-Perez, I. (2005). Perceptions of service providers and community members on intimate partner violence within a Latino community. *Health Education & Behavior*, 32(1), 69–83.

McAuliffe, W. E., Geller, S., LaBrie, R., Paletz, S., & Fournier, E. (1998). Are telephone surveys suitable for studying substance abuse? Cost, administration, coverage and response rate issues. *Journal of Drug Issues*, 28(2), 455–481.

McNeil, M., et al. (2006). Rapid community needs assessment after Hurricane Katrina—Hancock County, Mississippi, September 14–15, 2005. Centers for Disease Control, *MMWR Weekly*, 55(9), 234–236.

Milne, D.L., & Roberts, H. (2002). An educational and organizational needs assessment for staff training. *Behavioral and Cognitive Psychotherapy*, 30, 153–164.

Montcalm, D., & Royse, D. (2002). *Data analysis for social workers*. Boston: Allyn & Bacon.

McNeil, M., Goddard, J., Henderson, A., Phelan, M.S., Davis, S. & Wolkin, A. (2006). Rapid community needs assessment after Hurricane Katrina–Hancock County, Mississippi, September 14–15, 2005. *Morbidity & Mortality Weekly Report (MMWR)*, 55, 234–236.

Office of Applied Studies, 2003. *2003 National Survey on Drug Use and Health* http://oas.samhsa.gov/nhsda/2k3nsduh/2k3Overview.htm#toc

Penchansky, R. & Thomas, J. W. (1981). The concept of access: Definition and relationship to consumer satisfaction. *Medical Care*, 19 (2), 127–140.

Radloff, L.S. (1977). The CES-D Scale: A self-report depression scale for research in the general population. *Applied Psychological Measurement*, 3, 385–401.

Rowan-Szal, G. A., Greener, J. M., Joe, G. W., & Simpson, D. D. (2007). Assessing program needs and planning change. *Journal of Substance Abuse Treatment*, 33(2), 121–129.

Royse, D. (1987). Community perceptions of quality of care and knowledge of specific CMHC Services. *Journal of Marketing for Mental Health*, 1 (1), 151–166.

Royse, D. & Drude, K. (1982). Mental health needs assessment: Beware of false promises. *Community Mental Health Journal*, 18 (2), 97–106.

Royse, D. (2004). Research methods in social work. 4th Edition. Pacific Grove, CA: Brooks/Cole-Thomson.

Royse, D. (2008). *Research methods in social work*. 5th Edition. Belmont, CA: Thomson.

Rush, B. (1990). A systems approach to estimating the required capacity of alcohol treatment services. *British Journal of Addiction*, 85, 49–59.

Salize, H.J., et al. (2001). Needs for mental health care and service provision in single homeless people. *Social Psychiatry and Psychiatric Epidemiology*, 36, 207–216.

Sawicki, D. S. & Flynn, P. (1996). Neighborhood indicators: A review of conceptual and methodological issues. *Journal of the American Planning Association*, 62, 165–183.

Simons-Morton, B.G., Greene, W.H., & Gottlieb, N.H. (1995). *Introduction to health education and health promotion*. 2nd Edition. Prospect Heights, IL: Waveland Press.

Simpson, D.D. (2002). A conceptual framework for transferring research to practice. *Journal of Substance Abuse Treatment*, 27, 99–121.

Staton-Tindall, M., Havens, J., Leukefeld, C., & Burnette, C. (2007). Evaluation of Operation UNITE. Unpublished report, University of Kentucky Center on Drug & Alcohol Research.

The American Heritage® Dictionary of the English Language, 4th ed. Boston: Houghton Mifflin, 2000. www.bartleby.com/61/.

Tipping, J. (1998). Focus groups: A method of needs assessment. *The Journal of Continuing Education in the Health Professions, 18*, 150–154.

Tomkins, A., Shank, N., Tromanhauser, D., Rupp, S. & Mahoney, R. (2005). United Way and university partnerships in community-planning and plan implementation: The case of Lincoln/Lancaster County, Nebraska. *Journal of Community Practice*, 13 (3), 55–71.

Unruh, D. (2005). Using primary and secondary stakeholders to define facility-to-community transition needs for adjudicated youth with disabilities. *Evaluation and Program Planning, 28*, 413–422.

Vilela, M. (2007). Conducting interviews. The Community Tool Box. Retrieved November 14, 2007 from ctb.ky.edu.

Weinbach, R.W., & Grinnell, R.M. (1998). *Statistics for social workers*. 4th Edition. New York: Addison-Wesley Educational Publishers, Inc.

Weinbach, R.W., & Grinnell, R. M. (2007). *Statistics for social workers*. 7th Edition. Boston: Pearson Education, Inc.

Witkin, B. R. & Altschuld, J. W. (1995). *Planning and conducting needs assessments: A practical guide*. Thousand Oaks, CA: Sage Publications.

Index

CPSIA information can be obtained at www.ICGtesting.com
Printed in the USA
BVOW04s0355070414

349625BV00007B/26/P